YEAR IN SPORTS 2016

ISBN 978-0-545-82634-1

10 9 8 7 6 5 4 3 2 1   16 17 18 19

Printed in the U.S.A.   40
First edition, December 2015

Produced by Shoreline Publishing Group LLC

Cover design by Cheung Tai

Due to the publication date, records, results, and statistics are current as of August 2015.

Contents

Lots of Wows!

Why do you love sports? Is it to cheer for your favorite teams? Is it to watch athletes for tips on how to become a better competitor? Do you follow a team, a player, or a country? Or do you just watch to avoid doing homework?

Whatever reason you choose to watch sports, everyone loves those moments that just make you say "Wow!" You know, that instant when you see something you've never seen before happen right in front of your eyes. When you just have to say "Wow!" and then tell all your friends to watch the replay.

The past Year in Sports had plenty of Wow! moments, in hundreds of places all around the world. On just about every page inside, you'll look back on what made you jump up and shout. Of course, sometimes they might remind you of when the "other guys" did the shouting . . . sorry! That's the other thing about sports—you can't win 'em all.

One of the biggest Wows! of this past year came in a set of three. **Carli Lloyd** of the US women's soccer team scored a shocking three-goal hat trick in the World Cup final against Japan, giving America its third world title.

The sport of horseracing provided another tripleheader of Wows!, as **American Pharoah** became the first horse in 37 years to win the

Here's Lloyd scoring the second of her three goals in the final.

Triple Crown. As he pounded down the stretch to win the Belmont Stakes, Pharoah made history as he enjoyed the cheers—and Wows!—of millions of fans.

The Seattle Seahawks provided a gigantic Wow! in Super Bowl XLIX. Unfortunately, it was New England Patriots fans who said it after Seattle's **Russell Wilson** threw an interception on a play that would have given the Seahawks a second Super Bowl title. The pick instead made the Patriots four-time winners.

A pair of athletes in individual sports had seasons for the ages in 2015, creating a building series of Wows! Golfer **Jordan Spieth** had one of the greatest Grand Slam years ever, winning the US Open and the Masters, finishing second in the PGA Championship, and tying for fourth in the British Open. And he's only 21 years old! In

Spieth captured the US Open trophy in 2015.

women's tennis, **Serena Williams** dominated, capturing the Serena Slam (four straight Grand Slam championships, including one from 2014).

Look for those Wows! and these inside:

WOW!: Wisconsin knocked off undefeated Kentucky in the NCAA men's basketball tournament. **WOW!: Kevin Harvick** outdueled three other racers to capture NASCAR's Sprint Cup. **WOW!:** More than a billion people watched as Australia won the Cricket World Cup. **WOW!:** Ohio State's **Ezekiel Elliott** romped through the Oregon Ducks to help win the first College Football Playoff Championship. The Wows! go on and on. Dive in and see how many times you remember saying Wow! as you look at another truly amazing Year in Sports!

TOP 10

MOMENTS IN SPORTS
SEPTEMBER 2014 ▸ AUGUST 2015

To create this year's Top 10 list, we have traveled the world, seeking out the greatest and most amazing feats and events in sports. There is so much to choose from all around the globe, we couldn't just stick to the USA and expect to satisfy everyone.

More than ever before, American sports fans are paying close attention to what is happening on foreign fields, whether that means watching US women dominate in soccer or watching your family's ancestral home play championship cricket. Plus, fans enjoyed watching a pair of US athletes pack on the frequent flyer miles as they headed to faraway courts and courses to pick up championship hardware.

All this jet-setting and globetrotting is a great lead-in to what will surely be an amazing 2016, with the Summer Olympics beaming to every corner of the world from Rio de Janeiro. This space next year will surely be filled with gold-medal moments. Until then, let's cast a look backward at this eye-popping international edition of the Top Ten Moments in Sports!

10 HISTORIC HURLER

When you have to reach back 110 years for a comparison, you know you're watching something special. *Madison Bumgarner* of the 2015 San Francisco Giants made like Christy Mathewson of the 1905 New York Giants, who threw three shutouts in six days. All Bumgarner did was win two games, allow one run in 21 innings, and oh, yes, come in for a remarkable four-inning save in Game 7. The Giants won their third title in five years.

9 STREAK SNAPPERS *Would Kentucky be the latest team to "run the table" and win the NCAA tournament while going undefeated? The Wildcats moved through the early rounds like they would do just that. Then in the national semifinal, they met up with a stubborn Wisconsin team. The Badgers, led by* Frank "the Tank" Kaminsky *(44) ignored the record and snapped the Kentucky streak. Though Wisconsin lost to Duke in the final, they can point with pride to a historic victory.*

8 **CLASSIC CATCH** *Oh, yes he did! A rookie wide receiver who was doing pretty well suddenly became a national sensation with one amazing play. The Giants' Odell Beckham Jr. made this leaping, twisting, three-fingers-of-one-hand touchdown catch that lit up social media almost before he landed in the end zone. That was the biggest of his many big plays in a dynamic rookie season.*

ICC
CRICKET
WORLD

7 AWESOME AUSSIES *Cricket is a really, really big deal to an enormous number of people. It's just that very few of them live near you. In the spring of 2015, Americans and more than a billion others got to share in the fun as Australia won the ICC World Cup championship of cricket.*

ET WORLD CUP 2015 AUSTRALI

6

SERENA SLAM! *The Grand Slam of tennis means winning all four of the sport's major tournaments in the same year. Serena Williams invented her own kind of slam. With her dominating win at Wimbledon in 2015, she wrapped up the "Serena Slam" with four straight Grand Slam wins, a streak that started with the 2014 US Open. Few athletes today "own" their sports as much as Williams owns women's tennis.*

5 GREAT GOLFER *Jordan Spieth* has been lurking for about a year now. He was considered one of the best young golfing talents, and in 2015, he proved it. Spieth won the Masters (pictured here in the winner's green jacket) and the US Open and came within one shot of making it three majors in a row, losing the British Open by one stroke to *Zach Johnson*, before finishing second at the PGA Championship in August. By the end of the summer, he was the number one–ranked golfer in the world!

4

WARRIORS? WINNERS! *Take the best shooter in the NBA and surround him with a team that cares more for teamwork than stats, and you've got a winning formula. The Golden State Warriors, led by MVP sharpshooter Stephen Curry, held off the Cleveland Cavaliers—led by some guy named LeBron—to win their first NBA title since 1975.*

3

HISTORIC HORSE *Year after year, great Thoroughbred horses teased fans. The horses would win one or two legs of the Triple Crown and then fail in the Belmont Stakes. It happened six times just from 2002–2014 alone. Then came* American Pharoah. *Nothing stopped the powerful horse. His Belmont win for the Triple Crown broke a 37-year jinx.*

2 **SEAHAWKS SURPRISE** *One yard away. One play away. One Beast Mode blast up the middle away. That's how close the Seattle Seahawks were to becoming the first back-to-back Super Bowl champs since 2003. But from the New England Patriots' one-yard line, the team called a short pass play . . . and the Patriots'* Malcolm Butler (21) *intercepted the ball. That sealed the Pats' fourth Super Bowl victory, making* Tom Brady *a hero and* Russell Wilson, *who threw the pick, the goat.*

1 **WONDERFUL WOMEN!** *The US women's soccer team was under a lot of pressure. They were expected by most experts to win the Women's World Cup of soccer. In early games, however, the team struggled to score and looked less than outstanding. But in the knockout round, they rose up. Making the final against Japan, which had beaten the US in the 2011 final, America showed who was boss. Captain Carli Lloyd had a marvelous hat trick and the US dominated, winning 5-2. No more pressure!*

NFL

INSTANT HERO!

New England rookie cornerback Malcolm Butler put his name in Patriots history forever with this big interception. The pickoff kept the Seahawks from scoring in the last minute. New England held on to win its fourth Super Bowl, 28–24.

Off to the Races

Sometimes the NFL season is like a horse race . . . a very crowded horse race with enormous jockeys! It's a long way around the track, er, the season, and a lot can happen. Teams that break out of the pack early can fade as the season goes on. Teams that don't have a good start can end up among the leaders.

The 2014 season was a lot like that. What the season looked like at the start was a lot different from the end. And what an ending! The Super Bowl championship landed in the lap of one team after a controversial play!

In the season's first few weeks, the defending champion Seattle Seahawks and annual top team New England Patriots struggled. Neither team looked its best. Meanwhile, the up-and-coming Arizona Cardinals got off to a hot start. They won nine of their first ten games. It was the team's best start since 1947! The Dallas Cowboys also got off to a good start. A big reason was running back **DeMarco Murray**.

Murray left Dallas for Philadelphia in the off season.

He hustled for 100 or more yards in the first eight games of the season, setting a new NFL record. After losing their opening game, Dallas won six straight.

Detroit was another hot team early, with seven wins in their first nine games. A healthy **Calvin Johnson** was a big reason. The wide receiver missed part of 2013 and the Lions were happy he was back.

By the end of the regular season, some of the early stars were fading. Arizona was on its fourth quarterback, as injuries kept knocking out starter after starter. New England had roared back, as had Seattle. Green Bay was chugging along nicely, trying to keep pace with the still-hot Lions. The super-speed offense of the Philadelphia Eagles was getting a lot of help from its defense.

In the NFC South, no team had a winning record midway through the season . . . and it stayed that way. In the end, the Panthers made the playoffs with a 7-8-1 record. The AFC North, on the other hand, had three teams battling for playoff spots.

Out west, Seattle kept flying as the once-mighty San Francisco 49ers were grounded. In what would be coach **Jim Harbaugh**'s last season with the team, they lost four of their final five games and missed the playoffs. The Broncos, in the AFC West, were almost as dominant as they had been in 2013, when they won the conference title.

On the last weekend of the season, Green Bay ended up on top of the NFC North with a win over Detroit. Arizona squeaked into the playoffs even after losing their division title bid to Seattle. Carolina clinched the South with a thrashing of the Falcons.

Read about all the postseason games starting on page 24. Then see the complete Super Bowl coverage on page 26. You probably won't believe the story of that game. When 161.3 million people watched the game live, they didn't believe it either.

5

That's not a very big number, right? Then again, when it's the number of touchdowns scored by a defensive end . . . it's pretty huge! **J. J. Watt** scored three touchdowns catching passes. He also returned an interception and a fumble for scores. He was later the first player ever to get all the votes cast for NFL Defensive Player of the Year.

2014 Final Regular-Season Standings

AFC EAST	W	L	T
New England Patriots	12	4	
Buffalo Bills	9	7	
Miami Dolphins	8	8	
New York Jets	4	12	

AFC NORTH	W	L	T
Pittsburgh Steelers	11	5	
Cincinnati Bengals	10	5	1
Baltimore Ravens	10	6	
Cleveland Browns	7	9	

AFC SOUTH	W	L	T
Indianapolis Colts	11	5	
Houston Texans	9	7	
Jacksonville Jaguars	3	13	
Tennessee Titans	2	14	

AFC WEST	W	L	T
Denver Broncos	12	4	
Kansas City Chiefs	9	7	
San Diego Chargers	9	7	
Oakland Raiders	3	13	

NFC EAST	W	L	T
Dallas Cowboys	12	4	
Philadelphia Eagles	10	6	
New York Giants	6	10	
Washington Redskins	4	12	

NFC NORTH	W	L	T
Green Bay Packers	12	4	
Detroit Lions	11	5	
Minnesota Vikings	7	9	
Chicago Bears	5	11	

NFC SOUTH	W	L	T
Carolina Panthers	7	8	1
New Orleans Saints	7	9	
Atlanta Falcons	6	10	
Tampa Bay Buccaneers	2	14	

NFC WEST	W	L	T
Seattle Seahawks	12	4	
Arizona Cardinals	11	5	
San Francisco 49ers	8	8	
St. Louis Rams	6	10	

2014 Playoffs

Wild Card Playoffs

Cowboys 24, Lions 20

Dallas won its first playoff game since 2009 in a comeback against the Lions. **Tony Romo** hit **Terrance Williams** with the go-ahead score with less than three minutes to go. The Dallas D then sacked Detroit QB **Matthew Stafford** to seal the win.

Carolina 27, Arizona 16

Going into a playoff game with **Ryan Lindley**, a quarterback who has never won a game, is pretty tough. The Cardinals had to do that after injuries to their first two starters. The Carolina defense held Arizona to 78 total yards of offense, the least ever in an NFL playoff game.

Ravens 30, Steelers 17

Losing their starting running back a week before the playoffs hurt Pittsburgh. Without **Le'Veon Bell**, who had run for 1,361 yards to lead the AFC, the Steelers offense was quiet. Baltimore's **Joe Flacco** threw a pair of TD passes, while the Ravens' D recorded five sacks.

Colts 26, Bengals 10

QB **Andrew Luck** added another page to his amazing record by throwing a key TD pass while falling to the ground. He hit **Donte Moncrief** for the score that put Indy up by 10. For the Bengals, it was nothing new. This was the NFL-record fourth straight year they lost an opening-round playoff game.

Divisional Playoffs

Patriots 35, Ravens 31

In a great back-and-forth game, the Pats made the last big play. **Tom Brady** threw a scoring pass

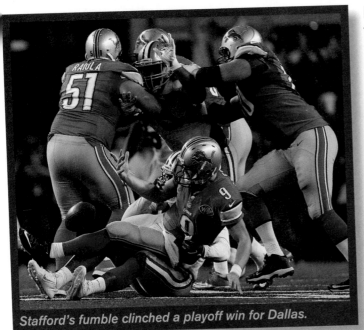

Stafford's fumble clinched a playoff win for Dallas.

to **Brandon LaFell** for the final points. It was Brady's NFL-record 46th TD pass in the postseason. The Patriots also became the first team to come back from 14 points down twice in one playoff game.

Colts 24, Broncos 13

Andrew Luck had two touchdown passes, while the Colts' D bottled up the Broncos' running game. Indy was the only team to win on the road this weekend.

Seahawks 31, Panthers 17

Big plays by Seattle (a 63-yard TD catch by **Jermaine Kearse** and a 90-yard pick-six by **Kam Chancellor**) joined a strong defense in sending the Seahawks back to the NFC Championship Game.

Packers 26, Cowboys 21

The Catch That Wasn't: **Dez Bryant** seemed to have made a catch at the 1-yard line that would have led to Dallas scoring a go-ahead TD. Instead, the call was reversed, Green Bay took over, and Dallas never got another chance.

Conference Championships

Seahawks 28, Packers 22

This game was over. The Packers had won it. But then they had to play the final three minutes. In one of the most shocking endings in recent seasons, Green Bay blew the lead and Seattle won in overtime. Seattle scored to make

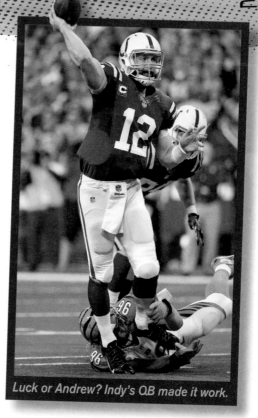

Luck or Andrew? Indy's QB made it work.

it 19–14 with about two minutes left. Then the Seahawks recovered the onside kick and drove down to score and take their first lead of the game. Green Bay wasn't done. **Aaron Rodgers** led them to a game-tying field goal, a 48-yarder by **Mason Crosby**. In overtime, **Russell Wilson** caught the Packers in the wrong defense and hit Kearse with the game-winning touchdown.

Patriots 45, Colts 7

New England was in control all the way. **Tom Brady** threw three touchdown passes and the Patriots were headed to their eighth Super Bowl, six of them under Brady's leadership. **LeGarrette Blount** added three rushing touchdowns in the game.

Really? A Pass Play?

SUPER BOWL XLIX · ARIZONA

When the dust of the playoffs settled, the Seattle Seahawks were back in the Super Bowl. They were the first team in 10 years to earn back-to-back trips to the big game. New England returned to their first Super Bowl since the 2011 season.

The Patriots spent most of the two weeks before this game answering questions about footballs . . . and physics.

Following the AFC Championship Game, it was revealed that New England's footballs did not have the right amount of air in them. Having less air would have made those footballs easier to throw and catch. It was a bother for Brady and friends, so they were happy when the game started.

The first quarter was scoreless, and then each team scored twice in the second. Brady's second TD pass was to super tight end **Rob Gronkowski**. Seattle tied it on the first NFL touchdown by **Chris Matthews**.

> **❝It was clutch time. I knew we needed it. So I just went in and made the play.❞**
>
> — NEW ENGLAND'S **MALCOLM BUTLER**

The third quarter was all Seattle. They got a field goal and a **Russell Wilson**-to-**Doug Baldwin** TD, and kept the Patriots scoreless. In Super Bowl history, no team had come back from 10 points behind in the fourth quarter.

Brady got right to work. First, he hit **Danny Amendola** on a short TD pass. After a 10-play, 64-yard drive, he threw a TD pass to **Julian Edelman**. It was the Patriots' first lead of the half.

But would it hold up? Seattle had one more shot.

A surprise pass to **Marshawn Lynch**, the stud running back who had lined up at receiver, took them to midfield. A moment later came one of the two

The Butler did it! This pick sealed a Patriots win.

SUPER TOM

Tom Brady won his third MVP award, tying **Joe Montana** (49ers) for the most ever. Brady also won the MVP after Super Bowls XXXVI and XXXVIII. For winning the award this year, Brady was given a new truck by a league sponsor. Brady is doing pretty well for himself and has plenty of vehicles. So he gave his new ride to another Super Bowl hero, rookie cornerback **Malcolm Butler**.

plays that you'll be talking about for years. Wilson lofted a ball to **Jermaine Kearse** along the right sideline. Kearse and New England's **Malcolm Butler** leaped to meet the ball. It was tipped in the air. Kearse tipped it again as he fell to the ground . . . and then hit it with both legs . . . and then, lying on his back, he snagged it to his chest. It was a miracle catch! Lynch nearly scored on the next play. Then came the play of the year . . . the biggest Super Bowl goof-up of all time, and the play that defined the season.

Instead of letting power back Lynch stuff it into the end zone to seal the win, Seahawks coach **Pete Carroll** called for a short pass play. What? No one could believe it was happening. Wilson got the snap and zinged a quick pass toward **Ricardo Lockette**. One big problem: Butler from New England was already there. He stepped up and made the interception heard 'round the world. Brady threw up his hands for joy on the sideline. Seattle fans could only stare in shock. Football fans everywhere shouted, "Why did you pass?!" One yard from winning back-to-back Super Bowls, the Seahawks blew it.

Brady finished off the game and earned his fourth Super Bowl ring as the Patriots won, 28–24, thanks to what most experts are calling the worst play in Super Bowl history.

SUPER BOWL XLIX

TEAM	1Q	2Q	3Q	4Q	FINAL
SEA	0	14	10	0	24
NE	0	14	0	14	28

SCORING

2Q: NE — B. LaFell 11 pass from T. Brady (Gostkoswki kick)

2Q: SEA — M. Lynch 3 rush (Hauschka kick)

2Q: NE — R. Gronkowski 22 pass from T. Brady (Gostkowski kick)

2Q: SEA — C. Matthews 11 pass from R. Wilson (Hauschka kick)

3Q: SEA — Hauschka 27 FG

3Q: SEA — D. Baldwin 3 pass from R. Wilson (Hauschka kick)

4Q: NE — D. Amendola 4 pass from T. Brady (Gostkowski kick)

4Q: NE — J. Edelman 3 pass from T. Brady (Gostkowski kick)

2014 Stats

1,845 RUSHING YARDS
DeMarco Murray, Cowboys

13 RUSHING TDS
DeMarco Murray, Cowboys
Marshawn Lynch, Seahawks

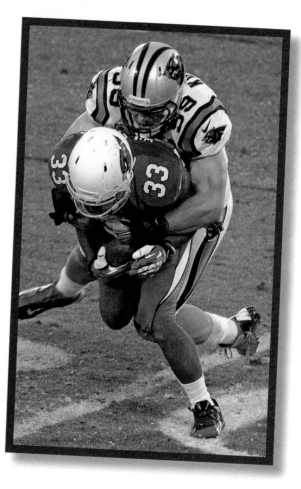

40 PASSING TDS
Andrew Luck, Colts

4,952 PASSING YARDS
Drew Brees, Saints
Ben Roethlisberger, Steelers

1,698 RECEIVING YARDS
129 RECEPTIONS
Antonio Brown, Steelers

16 RECEIVING TDS
Dez Bryant, Cowboys

35 FIELD GOALS
156 POINTS
Stephen Gostkowski, Patriots

◀◀◀**153** TACKLES
Luke Kuechly, Panthers

22 SACKS
Justin Houston, Chiefs

7 INTERCEPTIONS
Glover Quin, Lions

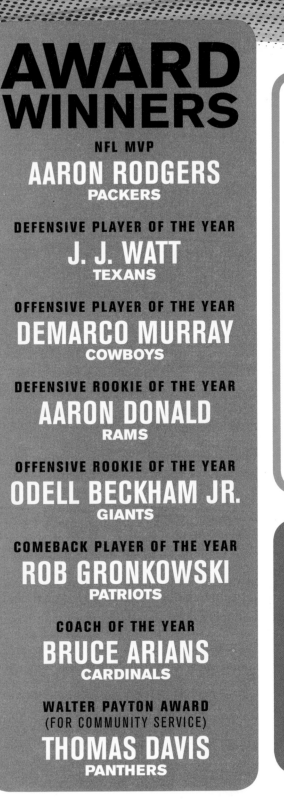

AWARD WINNERS

NFL MVP
AARON RODGERS
PACKERS

DEFENSIVE PLAYER OF THE YEAR
J. J. WATT
TEXANS

OFFENSIVE PLAYER OF THE YEAR
DEMARCO MURRAY
COWBOYS

DEFENSIVE ROOKIE OF THE YEAR
AARON DONALD
RAMS

OFFENSIVE ROOKIE OF THE YEAR
ODELL BECKHAM JR.
GIANTS

COMEBACK PLAYER OF THE YEAR
ROB GRONKOWSKI
PATRIOTS

COACH OF THE YEAR
BRUCE ARIANS
CARDINALS

WALTER PAYTON AWARD
(FOR COMMUNITY SERVICE)
THOMAS DAVIS
PANTHERS

Good Stuff!

Some impressive numbers from the 2014 NFL season:

* Pittsburgh's **Antonio Brown** caught 129 passes, second-most in a season all-time.

* Giants receiver **Odell Beckham Jr.**'s 1,305 receiving yards was the most ever by a player in his first 12 NFL games.

* Kansas City's **Justin Houston**'s 22 sacks were just 0.5 sacks behind the record.

* Baltimore's **Jacoby Jones** had his third TD of 105 yards or more, an NFL best.

* Philadelphia kicker **Cody Parkey**'s 150 points were the most scored by a rookie in NFL history.

160

That's how many regular-season wins New England's **Tom Brady** has through the 2014 season. He is only the third QB ever to reach that mark, joining **Brett Favre** (186) and **Peyton Manning** (179).

1st Quarter
NFL WEEKS 1-4

✶ Good Start, Rook!: Jacksonville receiver **Allen Hurns** became the first rookie ever with two receiving touchdowns in the first quarter of his first game. He ended the season with 6 TD catches.

✶ Comebacks! Part 1: Also in Week 1, the Eagles became the first team to trail 17-0 at the half . . . and win by 17! Philly scored 34 unanswered points in defeating Jacksonville, 34-17.

✶ Bad News/Good News: In Week 2, Washington starting quarterback **Robert Griffin III** went out with a dislocated ankle. But backup **Kirk Cousins** led his team to a 41-10 win over Jacksonville.

> **❝My first thought was, 'Where's my helmet?'❞**
>
> — WASHINGTON BACKUP QB **KIRK COUSINS**, AFTER STARTER ROBERT GRIFFIN III WAS HURT

◀◀◀ Many Happy Returns: In Week 3, Atlanta's **Devin Hester** became the NFL's all-time leader with 20 career touchdowns on returns (punt, kickoff, missed field goal, or interception). His 62-yard punt-return score was part of the Falcons' 56-14 romp over the Buccaneers.

✶ Super Bowl 48.5: It was only the sixth Super Bowl rematch ever. After Seattle whomped Denver in Super Bowl XLVIII, 43-8, this regular-season repeat was much more exciting. Seattle's defense bottled up **Peyton Manning** again, but the Seahawks' offense didn't get going, either. Manning rallied the Broncos for a game-tying touchdown and two-point conversion with just seconds left. But **Russell Wilson** got the ball in overtime and led the 'Hawks to the game-winning TD for a 26-20 win.

Happy Hester goes for six . . . again!

2nd Quarter
NFL WEEKS 5-8

✱ Comebacks! Part 2:
In Week 5, the Browns set an NFL record by coming back from 25 points behind on the road. They trailed at Tennessee, 28–3, before storming back in the second half to win 29–28. The same afternoon, Buffalo used a 58-yard field goal by **Dan Carpenter** to complete a smaller comeback against Detroit. And the Saints needed 11 fourth-quarter points to tie the Buccaneers. New Orleans won in overtime, 37–31.

Peyton's Place

Denver's **Peyton Manning** threw his 509th career touchdown pass in Denver's 42–17 win over San Francisco. That put him past **Brett Favre** into first place all-time for career scoring strikes. Manning ended the season with the new record of 530.

✱ The Other Eagles "Offense":
Philadelphia's fast-moving offense gets most of the headlines. But in its first five games, the Eagles scored a record-setting 7 touchdowns on defense and special teams.

✱ High Tie: In Week 6, the Panthers and Bengals tied at 37–37 after an overtime period in which they both kicked field goals. It was the most points ever scored in an NFL tie.

✱ Four for 400: October 26 was the first day in NFL history on which four passers threw for 400 or more yards. The list: **Ben Roethlisberger**, Pittsburgh (522 passing yards); **Aaron Rodgers**, Green Bay (418); **Nick Foles**, Philadelphia (411); and **Andrew Luck**, Indianapolis (400).

✱ Really Big Ben: Roethlisberger became only the second player ever with a pair of 500-yard, 6-TD games. He had 522 passing yards and those 6 scoring passes in the Steelers' 51–34 win over the Colts. That's 44.78 fantasy points for Big Ben's "owners," too! But wait . . . he did it again in Week 9, becoming the first player ever with back-to-back 6-TD games!

✱ Lucky in London: The Lions' **Matt Prater** missed a field goal that would have won the game over the Falcons. But a delay of game penalty allowed him to kick again . . . and he made it! The game was played in London, England.

✱ Quick Strike: Only 17 seconds into overtime, Minnesota linebacker **Anthony Barr** stripped the ball from Tampa Bay's **Austin Seferian-Jenkins**. Barr then returned the fumble for a game-winning TD, one of the quickest OT wins ever.

3rd Quarter
NFL WEEKS 9–12

✱ NFC Showdown: In Week 9, two of the top teams in the NFC to this point met, but only one came away on top. The Cardinals beat the Cowboys, 28–17. A big reason was how Arizona bottled up super-runner **DeMarco Murray**, who was held to a season-low 79 yards.

✱ Shocker in Miami: The Dolphins had been playing pretty well, but no one saw this coming. They shut out the Chargers, 37–0, holding San Diego runners to only 50 yards.

✱ Sweet Sixteen: Well, it was sweet for one half of the league's top QB rivalry—**Tom Brady** and **Peyton Manning**. The two superstars faced off for the sixteenth time, and Brady's Patriots came out on top, 43–21.

✱ High and Low: With a win over St. Louis, the Cardinals went to 8-1, the best record in the NFL. That was the first time the franchise had the league's best mark since 1966 and it was the first time it had started 8-1 since 1948! However, in the game, star QB **Carson Palmer** was lost for the season with a knee injury.

✱ Grounded Seahawks: In a Week 10 38–17 win over the Giants, Seattle QB **Russell Wilson** topped 100 yards rushing while teammate **Marshawn Lynch** ran for four TDs. That two-parter was an NFL first!

✱ A Day to Remember: New England rookie running back **Jonas Gray** had not scored a touchdown heading into his team's showdown with Indianapolis. When the dust settled, he had scored FOUR! They were a big reason the Pats won 42–20.

✱ Shocker in St. Louis: The Rams were 3-6 while the Broncos, led by **Peyton Manning**, were 7-2 and on a roll. Home cooking helped for St. Louis, which upset the AFC champs, 22–7. That means the Rams have beaten both of last season's Super Bowl teams!

◀◀◀ Hilton's Happy Day: Early on Sunday morning of Week 12, Colts receiver **T. Y. Hilton** watched his baby girl be born. That afternoon, he hauled in a 73-yard TD to help his team beat Jacksonville, 23–3. He took the football back to the hospital as his first present to his new baby!

4th Quarter
NFL WEEKS 13-17

✳ Watt's Up?:
Defensive end **J. J. Watt** is no stranger to cheers, but he's been getting them for a different reason this year. In Houston's Week 13, 45-21 win over Tennessee, Watt caught his third TD pass of the year! It was one of **Ryan Fitzpatrick**'s team-record six TD passes on the day. ▶▶▶

✳ Tough Times: The Giants and Jets were doing so poorly this year that the *New York Times* put out a story on Sunday in Week 14 suggesting other things to do than watch their hometown teams. Loyal Giants fans who stuck with them, however, saw their biggest win of the year, a 36-7 thrashing of the Titans.

✳ David Beats Goliath:
The Bills shocked the Packers in Buffalo, knocking off Green Bay 21-13. **Aaron Rodgers** had one of his worst days as a pro, as Buffalo picked off two of his passes and prevented him from throwing for any TDs.

✳ Field Goal Frenzy!: If you like kickers, then the Week 15 Cardinals-Rams game was for you. All the points came from field goals, the first such game since 2012. Arizona won, 4-2 (in field goals, 12-6 that is), to keep its NFC-best record.

✳ One More to Go: Carolina QB **Cam Newton** survived a scary car wreck with just a hurt back. He returned to help his Panthers beat Cleveland, 17-13, in Week 16. The win put them in position to make the playoffs with a final-game victory over Atlanta.

✳ Playoffs Start Early: Three games in the season's final weekend determined NFL division champions. And another gave a team a shot at a number-one playoff seed.

◉ Defense led the Panthers to a 34-3 win over the Falcons and gave Carolina the NFC South title. Carolina had a pair of pick-sixes in the game and six sacks.

◉ **Antonio Brown**'s punt-return TD sparked Pittsburgh to a win over Cincinnati. Both teams made the playoffs, but Pittsburgh became the AFC North champs.

◉ The Packers clinched the NFC North title and earned a first-round bye with their 30-20 win over Detroit.

◉ A 20-6 win by Seattle over St. Louis made the defending Super Bowl champs the No. 1 seed heading into the postseason.

More NFL News

750

With a win in Week 6 over the Falcons, the Bears became the first team in NFL history with 750 wins. That's all-time, of course, not just this season, and includes postseason wins!

Note that the Bears also played in Decatur, Illinois, while the Redskins played in Boston, too.

All-Time Wins by Team

CHICAGO BEARS	752
GREEN BAY PACKERS	740
NEW YORK GIANTS	691
PITTSBURGH STEELERS	618
WASHINGTON REDSKINS	592

Stats Stars

Some statistical highlights from the 2014 NFL season:

★ **DeMarco Murray** set a new Cowboys single-season rushing record (and led the NFL) with 1,845 yards. That topped the old team mark set in 1995 by NFL all-time leading rusher **Emmitt Smith**. **Dez Bryant** also broke a Dallas season record with 16 TD catches.

◄◄◄ **Matt Forté** of the Chicago Bears set a new NFL single-season record for receptions by a running back, with 102. He broke the old mark set by Arizona's **Larry Centers**.

★ Houston defensive star **J. J. Watt** became the first player to record a pair of 20-sack seasons. He had 20.5 in 2012 and 2014.

★ Peyton who? **Andrew Luck** reached 4,761 passing yards, the most ever by a Colts quarterback.

WORLD'S GREATEST CATCH! We have to give some room for another angle on this catch by Giants rookie receiver **Odell Beckham Jr.**, on November 24 (see Top 10, page 6). Twitter almost blew up as people reacted following his leaping, twisting, glue-fingered snag of a 43-yard TD pass against the Cowboys.

NFL Fantasy Stars

Odell Beckham Jr. made a lot of fantasy owners happy in 2014. Here are the top fantasy players at each position (based on NFL.com scoring).

POS.	PLAYER, TEAM	POINTS
QB	**Aaron Rodgers**, Packers	354.14
RB	**DeMarco Murray**, Cowboys	294.10
WR	**Antonio Brown**, Steelers	251.90
TE	**Rob Gronkowski**, Patriots	184.40
K	**Stephen Gostkowski**, Patriots	158.00
DEF	**Eagles**	177.00

2015 Hall of Fame

Welcome these new "residents" of Canton, Ohio, home of the Hall of Fame.

◀◀◀Junior Seau LB

A fierce tackler and fiery leader, Seau—who passed away in 2013—earned a record-tying 12 Pro Bowl bids for San Diego.

Will Shields G

A 12-time Pro Bowl player, he was named to the NFL's All-2000s Team, too.

Mick Tingelhoff C

He was a big part of the Vikings' four NFC championships.

Bill Polian

As a general manager, led three different teams (Bills, Panthers, Colts) to Super Bowl appearances.

Ron Wolf

Executive who helped guide the Raiders to two Super Bowl wins and the Packers to one in a career that lasted almost 40 years.

Jerome Bettis RB

"The Bus" rumbled for 13,662 yards in 13 seasons with the Steelers and Rams.

Tim Brown WR

His 1,094 career receptions are fifth-most all-time. He made nine Pro Bowls with the Raiders.

Charles Haley DE-LB

He won an NFL-record five Super Bowl rings with the Cowboys and 49ers and was a two-time NFL Defensive Player of the Year.

295

That's how many people have been inducted into the Pro Football Hall of Fame. The first class entered in 1963 and new greats of the game have joined their ranks ever since.

2015 NFL Season

NFL DRAFT TOP TEN

Here are the top ten picks in the 2015 NFL Draft. The big news was that quarterbacks went 1-2 overall for the first time since **Andrew Luck** and **Robert Griffin III** went there in 2012.

PICK	PLAYER/POSITION/SCHOOL	NFL TEAM
1.	**Jameis Winston**, QB, Florida St.	Buccaneers
2.	**Marcus Mariota**, QB, Oregon	Titans
3.	**Dante Fowler Jr.**, OLB, Florida	Jaguars
4.	**Amari Cooper**, WR, Alabama	Raiders
5.	**Brandon Scherff**, G, Iowa	Redskins
6.	**Leonard Williams**, DE, USC	Jets
7.	**Kevin White**, WR, West Virginia	Bears
8.	**Vic Beasley**, OLB, Clemson	Falcons
9.	**Ereck Flowers**, G, Miami	Giants
10.	**Todd Gurley**, RB, Georgia	Rams

PIONEER IN BLACK AND WHITE

The first female official in NFL history was set to take the field for the 2015 season. **Sarah Thomas**, a longtime line judge in the Big Ten, is the groundbreaker. Thomas worked her way up through high school games to become the first female to work a college football bowl game. She also got experience working with NFL teams at training camps. "I've had a lot of women tell me that they're going to start watching football," Thomas told nfl.com.

For the Record

Super Bowl Winners

GAME	SEASON	WINNING TEAM	LOSING TEAM	SCORE	SITE
XLIX	2014	**New England**	Seattle	28–24	Glendale, AZ
XLVIII	2013	**Seattle**	Denver	43–8	New Jersey
XLVII	2012	**Baltimore**	San Francisco	34–31	New Orleans
XLVI	2011	**NY Giants**	New England	21–17	Indianapolis
XLV	2010	**Green Bay**	Pittsburgh	31–25	Dallas
XLIV	2009	**New Orleans**	Indianapolis	31–17	South Florida
XLIII	2008	**Pittsburgh**	Arizona	27–23	Tampa
XLII	2007	**NY Giants**	New England	17–14	Glendale, AZ
XLI	2006	**Indianapolis**	Chicago	29–17	South Florida
XL	2005	**Pittsburgh**	Seattle	21–10	Detroit
XXXIX	2004	**New England**	Philadelphia	24–21	Jacksonville
XXXVIII	2003	**New England**	Carolina	32–29	Houston
XXXVII	2002	**Tampa Bay**	Oakland	48–21	San Diego
XXXVI	2001	**New England**	St. Louis	20–17	New Orleans
XXXV	2000	**Baltimore**	NY Giants	34–7	Tampa
XXXIV	1999	**St. Louis**	Tennessee	23–16	Atlanta
XXXIII	1998	**Denver**	Atlanta	34–19	South Florida
XXXII	1997	**Denver**	Green Bay	31–24	San Diego
XXXI	1996	**Green Bay**	New England	35–21	New Orleans
XXX	1995	**Dallas**	Pittsburgh	27–17	Tempe, AZ
XXIX	1994	**San Francisco**	San Diego	49–26	South Florida
XXVIII	1993	**Dallas**	Buffalo	30–13	Atlanta
XXVII	1992	**Dallas**	Buffalo	52–17	Pasadena

GAME	SEASON	WINNING TEAM	LOSING TEAM	SCORE	SITE
XXVI	1991	**Washington**	Buffalo	**37–24**	Minneapolis
XXV	1990	**NY Giants**	Buffalo	**20–19**	Tampa
XXIV	1989	**San Francisco**	Denver	**55–10**	New Orleans
XXIII	1988	**San Francisco**	Cincinnati	**20–16**	South Florida
XXII	1987	**Washington**	Denver	**42–10**	San Diego
XXI	1986	**NY Giants**	Denver	**39–20**	Pasadena
XX	1985	**Chicago**	New England	**46–10**	New Orleans
XIX	1984	**San Francisco**	Miami	**38–16**	Stanford
XVIII	1983	**LA Raiders**	Washington	**38–9**	Tampa
XVII	1982	**Washington**	Miami	**27–17**	Pasadena
XVI	1981	**San Francisco**	Cincinnati	**26–21**	Pontiac, MI
XV	1980	**Oakland**	Philadelphia	**27–10**	New Orleans
XIV	1979	**Pittsburgh**	Los Angeles	**31–19**	Pasadena
XIII	1978	**Pittsburgh**	Dallas	**35–31**	Miami
XII	1977	**Dallas**	Denver	**27–10**	New Orleans
XI	1976	**Oakland**	Minnesota	**32–14**	Pasadena
X	1975	**Pittsburgh**	Dallas	**21–17**	Miami
IX	1974	**Pittsburgh**	Minnesota	**16–6**	New Orleans
VIII	1973	**Miami**	Minnesota	**24–7**	Houston
VII	1972	**Miami**	Washington	**14–7**	Los Angeles
VI	1971	**Dallas**	Miami	**24–3**	New Orleans
V	1970	**Baltimore**	Dallas	**16–13**	Miami
IV	1969	**Kansas City**	Minnesota	**23–7**	New Orleans
III	1968	**NY Jets**	Baltimore	**16–7**	Miami
II	1967	**Green Bay**	Oakland	**33–14**	Miami
I	1966	**Green Bay**	Kansas City	**35–10**	Los Angeles

BUCKEYE BASHER!

Ohio State running back Ezekiel Elliott ran wild in the College Football National Championship. His four touchdowns led the Buckeyes to a 42–20 victory over Oregon.

COLLEGE FOOTBALL

It Worked!

The 2014 college football season was an experiment. After all the games were played and all the confetti was picked up, the results were: success! The first year of the College Football Playoffs was (unless you were a TCU fan) a big hit with fans and teams alike. In the past, different schemes had been used to find out who was the national champion. Sometimes, it was by a vote of writers or coaches. In recent years, it was a mix of computers and people. The Bowl Championship Series pitted the No. 1 and No. 2 teams—according to a mysterious formula—until 2013. In 2014, the NCAA finally created what many fans wanted: a real playoff.

Okay, there were only four teams in it, but still, look what happened: The team ranked No. 4 at the start of the whole thing wound up carrying home the big trophy.

Before the playoff plan started, one loss pretty much eliminated a team from any chance at the top, especially a loss late in the season. And in earlier years, being undefeated meant being No. 1. Both of those went out the window in the playoff, in which the top four teams are chosen by a panel of experts. As a result,

Trevone Boykin of TCU

2014 TOP 10
FINAL AP POLL

1. **Ohio State**
2. **Oregon**
3. **TCU**
4. **Alabama**
5. **Michigan State**
   Florida State
7. **Baylor**
8. **Georgia Tech**
9. **Georgia**
10. **UCLA**

AWARD WINNERS

HEISMAN MEMORIAL TROPHY (BEST PLAYER)
MAXWELL AWARD (OUTSTANDING PLAYER)
WALTER CAMP AWARD (PLAYER OF THE YEAR)
DAVEY O'BRIEN AWARD (QB OF THE YEAR)
JOHNNY UNITAS GOLDEN ARM (QB OF THE YEAR)
Marcus Mariota/OREGON ▶

DOAK WALKER AWARD (RUNNING BACK)
Melvin Gordon/WISCONSIN

FRED BILETNIKOFF AWARD (RECEIVER)
Amari Cooper/ALABAMA

DICK BUTKUS AWARD (LINEBACKER)
Eric Kendricks/UCLA

JOHN MACKEY AWARD (TIGHT END)
Nick O'Leary/FLORIDA STATE

JIM THORPE AWARD (DEFENSIVE BACK)
Gerod Holliman/LOUISVILLE

OUTLAND TROPHY (INTERIOR LINEMAN)
Brandon Scherff/IOWA

LOU GROZA AWARD (KICKER)
Brad Craddock/MARYLAND

Florida State, the defending champion, was 13-0, but ranked third in the final playoff poll. Alabama and Oregon each had one loss but were ranked Nos. 1 and 2. The big move was Ohio State, which crushed Wisconsin in the Big Ten Championship Game and jumped above TCU to earn the key fourth spot. (Sorry, TCU. Someone had to be No. 5.) The "final four" teams played off in exciting end-of-the-season games (see pages 50–51).

Getting to that final four saw the usual roller-coaster ride as teams rose and fell with every fumble, touchdown, or game-winning play. For a while it looked like upstarts Mississippi and Mississippi State might both make it into the final four, but key losses saw their title hopes disappear. Auburn made a run at a return to the championship game, but mighty Alabama put a stop to that move by their in-state rival. TCU and Baylor both probably earned some votes for the final four. As late as December 7, TCU was going to make it, but Ohio State's final-week Badger-bashing binge pushed the Horned Frogs out of the top four. It was a rockin' and rollin' season, and we count down the months on the following pages.

SEASON HIGHLIGHTS
August/September

A&M's Hill put on a record-breaking show.

➜ Up and Down in Division II: You have to wonder if the College of Faith team actually used eleven players. In their 71–0 loss to Tusculum, they gained –100 total yards, the lowest mark ever in an NCAA game. On the other side of the coin, Texas A&M–Commerce racked up a division-record 986 total yards while beating East Texas, Baptist, 98–20.

➜ Time to Start a New Streak: Notre Dame shut out Michigan, 31–0. That ended Michigan's streak of 365 games in which they had scored. It also ended a 100-plus-year rivalry between the two famous schools that included 42 games since 1887.

➜ Luck of the Irish: Penn State won its season opener, 26–24, on a last-play field goal. The game, against Central Florida, was played at Croke Park in Dublin, Ireland! **Christian Hackenberg** threw for 454 yards in the game, the first Penn State passer to ever top 400 yards in one contest.

➜ Keee-rack!: Idaho traveled to Florida, but only got in one play. The two teams waited three hours for a lightning storm to pass. They did the kickoff . . . and the lightning returned. Officials canceled the game for fans' and players' safety.

➜ Kenny Football: Texas A&M QB **Kenny Hill** made people forget about 2012 Heisman Trophy winner Johnny "Football" Manziel in a hurry. Hill set a school record with 511 passing yards as the Aggies stomped South Carolina, 52–28.

➜ Just Like Dad: UCLA came back to defeat Texas thanks to backup QB **Jerry Neuheisel**'s game-winning TD pass. Jerry's dad, **Rick**, was also a UCLA passer (as well as the team's former head coach).

➜ Ouch!: California was looking at its first win in the Pac-12 in more than two seasons when it led Arizona 31–13 heading into the fourth quarter. But in the final 15 minutes, the Wildcats scored a stunning 36 points, while the Golden Bears added only 14. Arizona won it on a 47-yard, final-play, Hail Mary touchdown catch.

➜ Running Wild in Wisconsin: **Melvin Gordon** ran for 253 yards and five touchdowns as Wisconsin smashed Bowling Green, 68–17. The Badgers' total of 644 rushing yards was a Big Ten record.

➡ **Can't Spell Mississippi Without a 1!:** For the first time in school history, Mississippi State was ranked No. 1 in the AP poll. They knocked off No. 2 Auburn to continue an amazing run. They went from unranked to No. 1 faster than any team in history.

➡ **Broken Scoreboard:** Washington State QB **Connor Halliday** set an NCAA record by passing for 734 yards in a game against California. He threw 6 touchdown passes and led his team to a superb 59 points. One problem: Cal scored 60 points.

➡ **Top 10 Shootout:** No. 5 Baylor beat No. 9 TCU, 61–58. The combined 119 points were the most ever in a game matching two top 10–ranked teams.

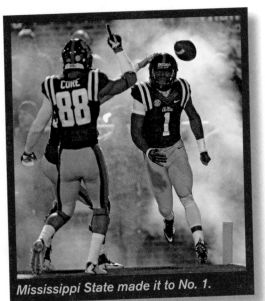
Mississippi State made it to No. 1.

➡ **Top 5 Showdown:** No. 2 Florida State needed a final-minute defensive stand—and a penalty on the Notre Dame offense—to keep the No. 5 Fighting Irish from scoring. The Seminoles remained one of three undefeated teams with a 31–27 win.

➡ **Well, That Was Quick:** Mississippi's time in the top 3 ended with an upset—a 10–7 loss to LSU. Ole Miss was in position for a game-tying field goal when LSU made a goal-line interception with just seconds left.

➡ **Really Big Passer:** Offensive linemen like 350-pound **Sebastian Tretola** rarely get the glory. But in Arkansas' win over Alabama–Birmingham, Tretola made a pass on a trick play . . . and hit wide receiver **Alan D'Appollonio** for a touchdown!

SATURDAY SHAKEUP

On October 4, the college football rankings took a beating. Teams ranked No. 2, 3, 4, 6, and 8 all lost, as did all the teams ranked from 14–19. The biggest news was No. 2 Oregon's loss to Arizona. No. 3 Alabama fell to Mississippi, and No. 4 Oklahoma lost to TCU. Mississippi State made it a clean sweep for that southern state by beating Texas A&M, ranked No. 6. When the dust cleared, the two Mississippi schools were tied for third in the country.

SEASON HIGHLIGHTS
November

➔ **Early Playoff Battle:** The first rankings of the College Football Playoff were announced before the November games. And as luck would have it, Nos. 3 and 4—Auburn and Mississippi—played on November 1. Auburn won when **Laquon Treadwell** was tackled and fumbled just before he could complete a game-winning score for Mississippi. He also broke his leg on the play. All in all, a bad ending for the Rebels.

➔ **Separation Saturday:** On November 8, four Top 10 teams lost, and probably fell out of a chance to make the College Football Playoff.

* No. 3 Auburn was upset by Texas A&M. Auburn fumbled twice in the last three minutes, including a botched snap when they were driving for a tying field-goal try.

* No. 7 Kansas State lost to No. 6 TCU, and it wasn't very close: 41–20.

* No. 8 Michigan State lost a Big Ten matchup to rival Ohio State, then ranked No. 14. That gave MSU two losses, and probably cost them a playoff spot.

* In another Top 10 matchup, No. 9 Arizona State made a big statement for the Pac-12, romping over No. 10 Notre Dame, 55–31.

➔ **Bama's Back:** An early-season loss to Mississippi knocked Alabama out of the playoff hunt . . . or did it? With a 25–20 win over No. 1 Mississippi State, the

Samaje Perine ran wild over the Jayhawks.

Crimson Tide leaped back into the national championship picture. They would use the game as a springboard into a spot in the final College Football Playoff.

➔ **Most Yards in a Game . . . Briefly:** On November 15, Wisconsin's **Melvin Gordon** set a single-game NCAA Division I record with 408 rushing yards. He broke a mark that had stood for almost 15 years. On November 22, Oklahoma's **Samaje Perine** broke that record, which Gordon had only owned for 7 days! Perine ran for 427 yards in a win over Kansas.

➔ **Old-School Football:** Lehigh and Lafayette will never be in the College Football Playoff or appear in a big bowl game. But they still play their games. In 2014, the two schools from Pennsylvania played for the 150th time. Lafayette won the latest game in a series that began back in 1884.

December

CONFERENCE CHAMPIONSHIPS

With the new College Football Playoff, the conference championship games were really the first round in those playoffs. Teams needed to take care of business and win their conference if they wanted to play in January.

Pac-12 Championship

Oregon manhandled No. 7 Arizona, 51–13—and it wasn't that close. The Ducks held on to their No. 2 ranking by overcoming the Wildcats' tough defense.

SEC Championship

Alabama left no doubts about its No. 1 ranking with a 42–13 thrashing of SEC East champ, Missouri.

Big Ten Championship

Behind third-string QB **Cardale Jones**—who took over after injuries to others—the Buckeyes shut out Wisconsin and star running back **Melvin Gordon**, 59–0. It was an impressive enough win that they leaped into the final four for the playoffs.

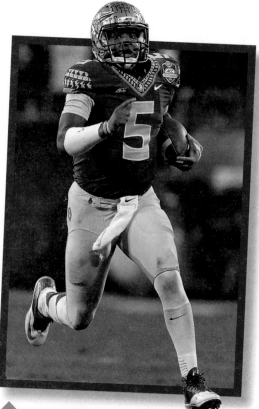

387

That's how many career receptions East Carolina senior **Justin Hardy** had for his college career. He set a new NCAA record, beating the old mark by 38!

▲▲ ACC Championship

Georgia Tech made it close, but Florida State held on to win, 37–35. That kept them undefeated and sent them into the final four. After so many tough wins, their players enjoyed a month off before they played Oregon in the Rose Bowl.

2014 Bowl Bonanza!

The College Football Playoff took over two of the biggest bowls. For the 2014 season, it was the Rose Bowl and the Sugar Bowl (page 50). That left plenty of other postseason bowl games for fans to enjoy. Here are some of the highlights (and lowlights!).

Miami Mix-Up

The Miami Beach Bowl between Memphis and BYU turned into the Beach Brawl. The two teams ended up fighting on the field after Memphis won 55–48 in double OT. The postgame handshake didn't go as planned, punches were thrown, and it took a while for officials to clear the field.

the island fans got a memorable ending. Central Michigan trailed Western Kentucky by 35 points in the second half but put on a huge rally. On the final play of the game, they used a long pass and three laterals to score a stunning 75-yard touchdown. The extra point would have tied the game, but Central decided to go for two . . . and didn't make it. Western Kentucky breathed a huge sigh of relief and won, 49–48.

◀ Crazy Comeback

Down by 25 in the fourth quarter, Houston rallied to beat Pittsburgh in the Armed Forces Bowl. It was the biggest fourth-quarter bowl-game comeback ever. Houston was helped by recovering not one but two onside kicks and then driving for scores. They clinched the *W* with a two-point conversion from **Greg Ward Jr.** to **Deontay Greenberry**.

Incredible Ending

In the Popeyes Bahamas Bowl (the first bowl game outside the US or Canada since 1937!),

Spartan!

It wasn't a Houston-level comeback, but it was still impressive. Michigan State scored three touchdowns in the final quarter of the Goodyear Cotton Bowl to upset No. 5 Baylor, 42–41. **Connor Cook** threw a TD pass with 17 seconds left for the victory.

QUIZ TIME

There are so many bowl games now, and the names are always changing. See how well you know your college football. From this list of bowls, circle the five that are not really bowl games after all!

Post Cereal Bowl

Duck Commander Independence Bowl

TaxSlayer Bowl

Monsanto Petunia Bowl

GottaEat.com Bowl

Belk Bowl

Quick Lane Bowl

NASA Astronaut Bowl

Gildan New Mexico Bowl

Florida Everglades Bowl

Badgers in OT

Wisconsin needed overtime to complete an upset win over Auburn in the Outback Bowl. Wisconsin kicked a field goal in overtime for a 34–31 win. It was a swan song for Badgers running back **Melvin Gordon**. He finished the season with 2,587 yards, second-most all-time.

Winning West

The Pac-12 had an amazing run in the bowl games. Utah, Arizona State, USC, Stanford, and UCLA all won their bowl games. Oregon won the Rose Bowl as part of the College Football Playoff. That gave the Pac-12 a superb 6-2 record, as only Arizona and Washington lost.

2014 PLAYOFFS
National Semifinals

Oregon 59, Florida State 20

The fast-moving Ducks blew out the undefeated Seminoles by 39 points. Florida State and star QB **Jameis Winston** lost their first game since November 2012 to Florida, as the Rose Bowl doubled as the first-ever College Football Playoff semifinal.

The game was actually sort of close at halftime, with Oregon up 18–13. But then FSU fumbled three times, and Winston tossed an interception. The worst was Winston's clumsy fumble that bounced right to a Duck player who rambled 58 yards for the score. Oregon scored 27 points in the third quarter and never looked back.

Oregon QB **Marcus Mariota** continued his Heisman Trophy–winning season with two TD passes and a TD run. For Winston, it was his first loss since he was a high school senior.

The Ducks set Rose Bowl records for yards gained (639) and points scored (59). And this was the 101st Rose Bowl Game!

Marcus Mariota

Ohio State 42, Alabama 35

Alabama, the No. 1 team in the College Football Playoff rankings, was upset by a determined Ohio State team. In only his second college start, OSU QB **Cardale Jones** was super, leading his team back from being behind 21–6 in the second quarter and 21–20 at halftime. A pair of Ohio State scores to start the second half, including an interception return by defensive end **Steve Miller**, put them ahead to stay. They sealed it with an 85-yard jaunt by running back **Ezekiel Elliott** in the fourth quarter.

The win by the Big Ten champions meant that, for the first time since 2005, an SEC team would not be part of the national championship game.

	1	2	3	4	F
OREGON	8	10	27	14	59
FLORIDA STATE	3	10	7	0	20

	1	2	3	4	F
OHIO STATE	6	14	14	8	42
ALABAMA	14	7	7	7	35

2014 CHAMPIONSHIP
Oregon vs. Ohio State

Talk about a deep bench. Ohio State was down to its third starting quarterback of the season. At the beginning of the 2014 campaign, **Cardale Jones** figured he might get a handful of snaps. Little did he know that he'd be making his third-ever start in the national championship game. He looked like a veteran, though, and led the Buckeyes to their fifth national title, beating Oregon, 42–20.

The first College Football Playoff Championship matched the No. 2 and No. 4 seeded teams, just like a real playoff can do. Against a solid Ohio State defense, Oregon's fast-moving offense never really got started. Meanwhile, Buckeyes running back **Ezekiel Elliott** was proving too much to handle. He rumbled for 246 yards and scored 4 touchdowns, averaging nearly 7 yards every time he got the ball. That was the highest total in a championship game since the start of the BCS back in 1998. For his part, Jones passed for a score and ran for another.

Oregon got to within a point in the third quarter, but then Jones drove OSU to 3 running TDs by Elliott to seal the championship. Ohio State also managed to overcome 4 turnovers.

Coach **Urban Meyer** became only the second man to win national titles at two schools. He also won a pair with Florida.

No. 3 was No. 1: Jones led OSU to the win.

The first year success of the playoff led many fans to start counting the days until the next one!

	1	2	3	4	F
OHIO STATE	14	7	7	14	42
OREGON	7	3	10	0	20

We're No. 1!

These are the teams that have finished at the top of the Associated Press's final rankings since the poll was first introduced in 1936.

SEASON	TEAM	RECORD	SEASON	TEAM	RECORD
2014	Ohio State	14–1	1974	Oklahoma	11–0
2013	Florida State	14–0	1973	Notre Dame	11–0
2012	Alabama	13–1	1972	USC	12–0
2011	Alabama	12–1	1971	Nebraska	13–0
2010	Auburn	14–0	1970	Nebraska	11–0–1
2009	Alabama	14–0	1969	Texas	11–0
2008	Florida	13–1	1968	Ohio State	10–0
2007	LSU	12–2	1967	USC	10–1
2006	Florida	13–1	1966	Notre Dame	9–0–1
2005	Texas	13–0	1965	Alabama	9–1–1
2004	USC	13–0	1964	Alabama	10–1
2003	USC	12–1	1963	Texas	11–0
2002	Ohio State	14–0	1962	USC	11–0
2001	Miami	12–0	1961	Alabama	11–0
2000	Oklahoma	13–0	1960	Minnesota	8–2
1999	Florida State	12–0	1959	Syracuse	11–0
1998	Tennessee	13–0	1958	LSU	11–0
1997	Michigan	12–0	1957	Auburn	10–0
1996	Florida	12–1	1956	Oklahoma	10–0
1995	Nebraska	12–0	1955	Oklahoma	11–0
1994	Nebraska	13–0	1954	Ohio State	10–0
1993	Florida State	12–1	1953	Maryland	10–1
1992	Alabama	13–0	1952	Michigan State	9–0
1991	Miami	12–0	1951	Tennessee	10–1
1990	Colorado	11–1–1	1950	Oklahoma	10–1
1989	Miami	11–1	1949	Notre Dame	10–0
1988	Notre Dame	12–0	1948	Michigan	9–0
1987	Miami	12–0	1947	Notre Dame	9–0
1986	Penn State	12–0	1946	Notre Dame	8–0–1
1985	Oklahoma	11–1	1945	Army	9–0
1984	Brigham Young	13–0	1944	Army	9–0
1983	Miami	11–1	1943	Notre Dame	9–1
1982	Penn State	11–1	1942	Ohio State	9–1
1981	Clemson	12–0	1941	Minnesota	8–0
1980	Georgia	12–0	1940	Minnesota	8–0
1979	Alabama	12–0	1939	Texas A&M	11–0
1978	Alabama	11–1	1938	Texas Christian	11–0
1977	Notre Dame	11–1	1937	Pittsburgh	9–0–1
1976	Pittsburgh	12–0	1936	Minnesota	7–1
1975	Oklahoma	11–1			

NATIONAL CHAMPIONSHIP GAMES

Until 2014, there was no national championship playoff system in Division I college football. From 1998–2013, the NCAA tried the Bowl Championship Series, but that used computers and polls to come up with a final game that pitted No. 1 against No. 2. The new system, called the College Football Playoff, uses a panel of experts who set up a pair of semifinals that determine who plays for the national title. Ohio State won the first College Football Playoff. Here are the results of BCS and Playoff finals in the 2000s.

SEASON	SCORE	SITE
2014	**Ohio State 42, Oregon 20**	ARLINGTON, TX
2013	**Florida State 34, Auburn 31**	PASADENA, CA
2012	**Alabama 42, Notre Dame 14**	MIAMI, FL
2011	**Alabama 21, LSU 0**	NEW ORLEANS, LA
2010	**Auburn 22, Oregon 19**	GLENDALE, AZ
2009	**Alabama 37, Texas 21**	PASADENA, CA
2008	**Florida 24, Oklahoma 14**	MIAMI, FL
2007	**LSU 38, Ohio State 24**	NEW ORLEANS, LA
2006	**Florida 41, Ohio State 14**	GLENDALE, AZ
2005	**Texas 41, USC 38**	PASADENA, CA
2004	**USC 55, Oklahoma 19**	MIAMI, FL
2003	**LSU 21, Oklahoma 14**	NEW ORLEANS, LA
2002	**Ohio State 31, Miami 24 (2 OT)**	TEMPE, AZ
2001	**Miami 37, Nebraska 14**	PASADENA, CA
2000	**Oklahoma 13, Florida State 2**	MIAMI, FL

MLB

CAIN YOU SAY "SAFE"?
Kansas City outfielder Lorenzo Cain helped his team reach the 2014 World Series. He and the Royals continued their stellar play in 2015, having the best record in the American League for most of the season as they worked toward another shot at the championship. Read more about the 2014 Series and 2015 highlights . . . inside!

2014: Season of Surprises

Winning lots of games in the regular season is very, very important. You can't have a shot at the World Series unless you win enough to make the playoffs. In 2014, several teams did a good job of winning lots and lots of games. They did not, however, do a very good job when it came to playoff time.

Some teams headed into the postseason for the first time in a long time. The Kansas City Royals had not made the playoffs since 1985!

One of the biggest surprises of the 2014 season was the play of the Baltimore Orioles. The O's won the AL East for the first time since 1997. That's not bad in a division that includes the mighty New York Yankees and the defending champion Boston

Is Mike Trout the best player in the game?

Red Sox. Boston fans will want to forget 2014. The team set a record by becoming the first club to go from worst (2012) to first (2013) to worst (2014). That left room for other new faces. Along with the Royals and Orioles, the Angels returned to the playoffs by winning the AL West. They had the best record in the Major Leagues helped by MVP **Mike Trout**. Even with all that talent and those wins, the Angels collapsed in the playoffs, where they were swept by the surprising Royals.

In the National League, the Brewers nearly made it back to the postseason. They were in first place in the NL Central for most of the year, but let the Cardinals and Pirates back in with a poor September. Led by their awesome

BYE-BYE BUD

The 2014 season marked the last for Commissioner **Bud Selig**. He had run baseball since 1992, one of the longest-serving commissioners ever. He helped create the very popular MLB.com and At Bat, the app that goes with it. He made the All-Star Game count for World Series home field, and he expanded the playoffs. The former Brewers owner retired in January and **Rob Manfred** took over as the tenth commissioner in baseball history.

2014 FINAL STANDINGS

AL EAST

Baltimore Orioles	96-66
New York Yankees	84-78
Toronto Blue Jays	83-79
Tampa Bay Rays	77-85
Boston Red Sox	71-91

AL CENTRAL

Detroit Tigers	90-72
Kansas City Royals	89-73
Cleveland Indians	85-77
Chicago White Sox	73-89
Minnesota Twins	70-92

AL WEST

Los Angeles Angels	98-64
Oakland Athletics	88-74
Seattle Mariners	87-75
Houston Astros	70-92
Texas Rangers	67-95

NL EAST

Washington Nationals	96-66
Atlanta Braves	79-83
New York Mets	79-83
Miami Marlins	77-85
Philadelphia Phillies	73-89

NL CENTRAL

St. Louis Cardinals	90-72
Pittsburgh Pirates	88-74
Milwaukee Brewers	82-80
Cincinnati Reds	76-86
Chicago Cubs	73-89

NL WEST

Los Angeles Dodgers	94-68
San Francisco Giants	88-74
San Diego Padres	77-85
Colorado Rockies	66-96
Arizona Diamondbacks	64-98

Kershaw dominated for the Dodgers.

starting pitchers, the Washington Nationals won the most games in the league. They were followed closely the the NL West champion Los Angeles Dodgers.

Like the Angels, however, both those top NL teams lost early in the playoffs, a pair of sudden endings to what had been great seasons.

The Dodgers' ace **Clayton Kershaw** had one of the best pitching seasons of all time. He became the first player to win both the MVP and Cy Young Awards for the National League since **Bob Gibson** in 1968!

All the action of the regular season stopped once the playoffs began. Of the teams that made the divisional series, the San Francisco Giants had the worst regular-season record. But in October, everyone started out 0-0 all over again. Thanks to some of the best postseason pitching of all time, the Giants ended up on top for the third time in five seasons. Read all about it on page 60.

2014 Postseason

The Orioles flew into the ALCS.

(**Max Scherzer**, **Justin Verlander**, **David Price**) to sweep the Tigers.

NLDS

→ The Dodgers started eventual Cy Young and MVP winner **Clayton Kershaw**. The Cardinals didn't care. They knocked LA out of the playoffs for the second straight season.

→ After surviving the longest postseason game ever—18 innings in six hours, 23 minutes—the Giants beat the Nationals in four games.

ALDS

→ The Royals beat the Angels in three straight, including a pair of 11-inning wins. The Angels had come into the series with MLB's best regular-season record.

→ The Baltimore Orioles beat three Cy Young Award winners in a row

WILD CARD PLAYOFF

AL: The Kansas City Royals got their wild postseason off to a roaring start. Down by one in extra innings, they scored a pair of runs in the bottom of the 12th inning to knock off the A's.

NL: In another preview of the World Series, the Giants' **Madison Bumgarner** twirled a 4-hit shutout to send the Pirates home.

2014 Championship Series

ALCS

The Orioles were the surprise winners of the AL East, while the Royals were a surprise just to be in the playoffs. The series opened in Baltimore and the Royals won both games there. After winning three extra-inning games earlier in the postseason, they won Game 1 in 10 innings. That gave them a record four wins with extra frames. In Game 4, KC went for the sweep. They got two runs in the first and made them stand up, thanks in part to great defense from outfielders **Alex Gordon** and **Lorenzo Cain**. Defense was a big part of the Royals' success, with just about every player contributing a big play. For his catches and timely hitting, Cain, in center field, was named the ALCS MVP. The sweep gave the Royals wins in their first eight games in the playoffs, an all-time record.

NLCS

Most pitchers don't like to pitch on the road, and certainly not in big games. For San Francisco's **Madison Bumgarner** . . . no problem. He pitched 7 2/3 shutout innings in Game 1 to extend a career scoreless streak to more than 26 innings. That was a new Major League record for road playoff games. **Kolten Wong** hit a walk-off homer for St. Louis to even the series. A Cardinals error gave the Giants their own walk-off win in Game 3. **Buster Posey** had 3 RBI as the Giants won Game 4. In Game 5, Bumgarner again pitched well (he was the series MVP) and the teams were tied 3–3 in the ninth. As Giants fans roared with delight, outfielder **Travis Ishikawa** slammed a three-run homer to win the game and the series. It would be the third trip to the Fall Classic in five seasons for San Francisco.

Kansas City's Lorenzo Cain sparkled in the field and at the plate as the Royals romped.

Madison's Moment
2014 WORLD SERIES

Your older relatives probably tell you about some of the great pitching performances in World Series history. There was Sandy Koufax in 1965. Bob Gibson in 1968. Jack Morris in 1991. Or you can read about things even older: Lew Burdette in 1957, Christy Mathewson in 1905! Well, now you'll be able to add another story to that list. You can tell your grandchildren you saw Madison Bumgarner pitch in the World Series. The Giants' lefty put on one of the finest performances in baseball history. He pitched in three games of the seven-game series and did more than anyone to end the Royals' Cinderella season.

World Series hero Madison Bumgarner

52 1/3

That's how many innings Bumgarner threw in the 2014 postseason. Amazingly, he had just a 1.03 ERA. He struck out seven batters for every batter he walked. His final five-inning save was one for the ages. He was the first pitcher since 1908 to get two wins and a save of three or more innings in relief.

GAME 1 The Giants had the worst regular-season record . . . and the best possible start to a World Series. They scored three runs in the first inning off the Royals ace, James Shields. Madison Bumgarner started and went 7 2/3. The home run he gave up for the Royals' only run would be the last score he would give up in 2014.

GAME 2 A five-run sixth inning clinched this game for the Royals. A two-run double by Salvador Perez and a home run by Omar Infante were the big hits. Rookie pitcher Yordano Ventura had a solid start for Kansas City.

GAME 3 The Royals had been doing very well on the road in the postseason and they continued that trend. After taking a 3–2 lead after six innings, they called on their bullpen. It delivered. Brandon Finnegan, Wade

Davis, and **Greg Holland** didn't let the Giants come back.

GAME 4 **Hunter Pence** was the hitting star for the Giants in this big win to tie the Series, but he had help. San Francisco scored a Series-high 11 runs, helped by three RBI from Pence and a pair from **Pablo "Kung Fu Panda" Sandoval** and **Joe Panik**. They needed the bats after Giants starter **Ryan Vogelsong** gave up four runs in three innings.

GAME 5 With pitchers like **Bumgarner**, who needs defense? The great lefty earned his second win of the Series with a four-hit shutout. A three-run eighth, helped by **Juan Perez's** two-run double, clinched the game for the Giants.

GAME 6 The Giants' hopes of clinching the World Series title in this game disappeared early. **Jake Peavy** and **Yusmeiro Petit** combined to give up seven runs in the first two innings. Outfielder **Lorenzo Cain** had three RBI for Kansas City in the romp.

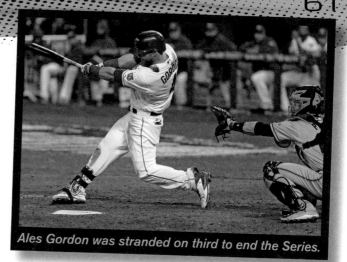
Ales Gordon was stranded on third to end the Series.

GAME 7 It all came down to Game 7. Should **Bumgarner** start this game for the Giants? It had only been two days since his great shutout. Some fans wanted him out there from the start. Manager **Bruce Bochy** decided to keep his ace in reserve and give **Tim Hudson** a chance. It didn't work. The Royals got to him early. Reliever **Jeremy Affeldt** kept the Royals quiet, and when the Giants took a 3–2 lead, Bochy called for his big lefty. Bumgarner threw five innings of shutout baseball to earn the save. Inning after inning, he went back out and shut 'em down. The Giants became the first NL team with three titles in five years since the 1946 St. Louis Cardinals!

WORLD SERIES 2014 RESULTS

GAME	SCORE	WP	LP
GAME 1	Giants 7, Royals 1	Bumgarner	Shields
GAME 2	Royals 7, Giants 2	Herrera	Peavy
GAME 3	Royals 3, Giants 2	Guthrie	Hudson
GAME 4	Giants 11, Royals 4	Petit	Finnegan
GAME 5	Giants 5, Royals 0	Bumgarner	Shields
GAME 6	Royals 10, Giants 0	Ventura	Peavy
GAME 7	Giants 3, Royals 2	Affeldt	Guthrie

Award Winners

MOST VALUABLE PLAYER

AL: **Mike Trout**
ANGELS

NL: **Clayton Kershaw**
DODGERS

CY YOUNG AWARD

AL: **Corey Kluber**
INDIANS

NL: **Clayton Kershaw**
DODGERS

Slugging rookie star Jose Abreu

ROOKIE OF THE YEAR

AL: **Jose Abreu**
WHITE SOX

NL: **Jacob deGrom**
METS

MANAGER OF THE YEAR

AL: **Buck Showalter**
ORIOLES

NL: **Matt Williams**
NATIONALS

HANK AARON AWARD

AL: **Mike Trout**
ANGELS

NL: **Giancarlo Stanton**
MARLINS

ROBERTO CLEMENTE AWARD
(FOR COMMUNITY SERVICE)

Paul Konerko
WHITE SOX

Jimmy Rollins
PHILLIES

Stat Champs

AL Hitting Leaders

40 HOME RUNS
Nelson Cruz, Orioles

111 RBI
Mike Trout, Angels

.341 BATTING AVERAGE
225 HITS
56 STOLEN BASES
Jose Altuve, Astros

NL Hitting Leaders

37 HOME RUNS
Giancarlo Stanton, Marlins

116 RBI
Adrian Gonzalez, Dodgers

.319 BATTING AVERAGE
Justin Morneau, Rockies

184 HITS
Ben Revere, Phillies
Denard Span, Nationals

64 STOLEN BASES
Dee Gordon, Dodgers

AL Pitching Leaders

18 WINS
Jered Weaver, Angels
Corey Kluber, Indians
Max Scherzer, Tigers

2.14 ERA
Felix Hernandez, Mariners

271 STRIKEOUTS
David Price, Rays/Tigers

Stanton turned his homers into big dollars!

48 SAVES
Fernando Rodney, Mariners

NL Pitching Leaders

21 WINS
1.77 ERA
Clayton Kershaw, Dodgers

242 STRIKEOUTS
Stephen Strasburg, Nationals
Johnny Cueto, Reds

47 SAVES
Craig Kimbrel, Braves

2014 MLB Notes

◀◀◀ Last-Day No-No

Washington's **Jordan Zimmermann** (shown here under a shaving cream–pie celebration) capped off the Nationals' division-winning season with the first no-hitter for the franchise since 1991. He was saved by a ninth-inning diving grab by rookie outfielder **Steven Souza Jr.**

Super Cy!

Clayton Kershaw walked away with the NL Cy Young and MVP awards after a magical 2014 season. He started 27 games and allowed three runs or fewer in all but one of them, or 96 percent. That was the best by any pitcher since 1900! He led the NL with 21 wins and led the Majors with a 1.77 ERA.

A Giant Streak

Game after game, batters faced San Francisco's **Yusmeiro Petit**. Game after game, he got them out. Over the course of eight games, he retired 46 straight batters. That set a new Major League record!

He Hits, Too!

Madison Bumgarner had a pretty good World Series (page 60). He also had a good day on July 13. He and **Buster Posey** each hit grand slams. That was the first time in baseball history that a pitcher-catcher combo did that in the same game!

That Man Again

The Oakland A's hated seeing **Jerome Williams** on the mound, no matter what uniform he was wearing. In 2014, he beat the A's three times while pitching for three different teams—Houston, Texas, and Philadelphia. No pitcher had done that since at least 1900.

Stick to It!

Here's a story for people who know that hard work pays off. In September, **Guilder**

37,441

That mighty wind you might have felt all season came from big-league hitters. They set a new all-time record by whiffing 37,441 times. Pitchers loved all the free swinging, as more players are swingin' for the fences.

Rodriguez got a base hit for the Texas Rangers. Why the big deal? It was his first in the Major Leagues after spending 13 seasons as a full-time minor leaguer. "This is one of the best moments of my life," said Rodriguez. "My first big league hit, my first RBI, my father in the stands, my wife."

K Is for Cleveland ▶▶▶

The Indians' pitching staff, led by Cy Young winner **Corey Kluber**, gave their defense a rest. They set a Major League record with 1,450 strikeouts on the season.

One Last K Note

Twins right-hander **Phil Hughes** broke MLB's single-season strikeout-to-walk ratio, striking out 186 batters and walking just 16 for an 11.63 ratio to surpass **Bret Saberhagen's** 1994 mark of 11.00.

Great Send-off

Derek Jeter, the Yankees' longtime shortstop, hung up his glove after the 2014 season. He went out in dramatic fashion. In his final home at-bat, he delivered a game-winning single. Next stop: Cooperstown and the Hall of Fame.

Big Dude

Though he stands only 5'6", second baseman **Jose Altuve** of the Houston Astros was the big man in the lineup in 2014. He led the AL in batting, going 2-for-4 on the final day to clinch the crown. His 47 doubles, 225 hits, and 56 steals also were tops in the league.

Around the Bases 2015

✳ Practice, Practice: Any kids out there who wonder why practicing and doing your best at sports is a good idea, check out **Giancarlo Stanton**. The 25-year-old slugger, who led the NL in homers in 2014, signed the biggest deal in Major League history: $325 million to play for the Miami Marlins for 13 years.

Can He Pitch Underwater, Too?

Ambidextrous means being able to use both hands equally well. In June, Oakland A's pitcher **Pat Venditte** achieved a rare feat—he pitched both lefty and righty in the same inning! Wearing a special glove that works on either hand, the reliever had to announce to the hitter which arm he would use. (A newspaper headline writer's work went viral when he wrote that Oakland's new pitcher was "Amphibious.")

✳ Great Start! The Dodgers' **Adrian Gonzalez** broke out of the starting gate in 2015 in a big way. He had a home run in the team's first two games, and then hit three in the third game. His five dingers in three starts to begin a season set a new Major League record.

✳ Silent Stadium: Total attendance at the April 29 White Sox at Orioles game? Zero. For the first time in recorded baseball history, a pro game was played with no fans in the stands. Following a protest in the streets around Oriole Park at Camden Yards, one game was suspended. MLB decided to play the next game with no fans, since there seemed to be no time later in the season to reschedule. So the hits and pitches echoed in an empty stadium.

✳ Big Bat in Chicago: One of the most-anticipated rookies in years joined the Chicago Cubs. Third baseman **Kris Bryant** hit 43 homers in the minors in 2014, and Cubs fans could not wait to see what he could do at Wrigley Field. Though he struck out three times in his debut, he caught on quickly. He had 31 RBI in his first 38 games. Among his 10 homers through June was a mammoth 477-foot blast that smacked into the Cubs' new video board in centerfield.

Feats:

◎ Tampa Bay pitcher **Chris Archer** became the first player since 1900 to have three straight games with 15 strikeouts and no walks.

◎ Dodgers catcher **Yasmani Grandal** had eight RBI, thanks in part to a pair of three-run homers, in a 14–4 win over the Brewers.

◎ Yankee DH **Alex Rodriguez** made his 3,000th career hit a special one, slugging a homer to right. His 3,001st was a long ball, too!

◀◀ Washington's ace **Max Scherzer** was one strike away from a perfect game when he hit Pittsburgh's **José Tábata**. Scherzer did get his no-hitter.

2015 Hall of Fame Class

For the first time in Hall of Fame history (the first class was elected way back in 1936!), three pitchers will join the Hall in the same year.

CRAIG BIGGIO: ◆ Played catcher, second base, and outfield in 20 years with Houston Astros ◆ 3,060 career hits ◆ 668 doubles: most all-time by right-handed batter ◆ Only player ever with at least 3,000 hits, 600 doubles, 400 stolen bases, and 250 home runs.

RANDY JOHNSON: ◆ Flame-throwing lefty won five Cy Young Awards ◆ Second all-time with 4,875 strikeouts ◆ Led league in strikeouts nine times and has five of the top 11 season strikeout totals ◆ Co-MVP of 2001 World Series.

PEDRO MARTÍNEZ: ▶▶▶

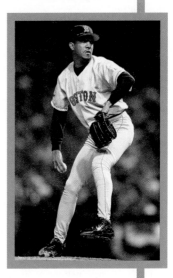

◆ Helped the Red Sox win 2004 and 2007 World Series ◆ Won three Cy Young Awards ◆ Won pitching Triple Crown in 1999 ◆ Native of Dominican Republic.

JOHN SMOLTZ: ◆ Multitalented pitcher; only player with 200 wins and 150 saves ◆ Helped Atlanta reach the playoffs every year from 1991–2005 (except when injured in 2000) ◆ Won 1996 Cy Young Award.

World Series Winners

YEAR	WINNER	RUNNER-UP	SCORE*	YEAR	WINNER	RUNNER-UP	SCORE*
2014	San Francisco Giants	Kansas City Royals	4-3	1987	Minnesota Twins	St. Louis Cardinals	4-3
2013	Boston Red Sox	St. Louis Cardinals	4-2	1986	New York Mets	Boston Red Sox	4-3
2012	San Francisco Giants	Detroit Tigers	4-0	1985	Kansas City Royals	St. Louis Cardinals	4-3
2011	St. Louis Cardinals	Texas Rangers	4-3	1984	Detroit Tigers	San Diego Padres	4-1
2010	San Francisco Giants	Texas Rangers	4-1	1983	Baltimore Orioles	Philadelphia Phillies	4-1
2009	New York Yankees	Philadelphia Phillies	4-2	1982	St. Louis Cardinals	Milwaukee Brewers	4-3
2008	Philadelphia Phillies	Tampa Bay Rays	4-1	1981	Los Angeles Dodgers	New York Yankees	4-2
2007	Boston Red Sox	Colorado Rockies	4-0	1980	Philadelphia Phillies	Kansas City Royals	4-2
2006	St. Louis Cardinals	Detroit Tigers	4-1	1979	Pittsburgh Pirates	Baltimore Orioles	4-3
2005	Chicago White Sox	Houston Astros	4-0	1978	New York Yankees	Los Angeles Dodgers	4-2
2004	Boston Red Sox	St. Louis Cardinals	4-0	1977	New York Yankees	Los Angeles Dodgers	4-2
2003	Florida Marlins	New York Yankees	4-2	1976	Cincinnati Reds	New York Yankees	4-0
2002	Anaheim Angels	San Francisco Giants	4-3	1975	Cincinnati Reds	Boston Red Sox	4-3
2001	Arizona Diamondbacks	New York Yankees	4-3	1974	Oakland Athletics	Los Angeles Dodgers	4-1
2000	New York Yankees	New York Mets	4-1	1973	Oakland Athletics	New York Mets	4-3
1999	New York Yankees	Atlanta Braves	4-0	1972	Oakland Athletics	Cincinnati Reds	4-3
1998	New York Yankees	San Diego Padres	4-0	1971	Pittsburgh Pirates	Baltimore Orioles	4-3
1997	Florida Marlins	Cleveland Indians	4-3	1970	Baltimore Orioles	Cincinnati Reds	4-1
1996	New York Yankees	Atlanta Braves	4-2	1969	New York Mets	Baltimore Orioles	4-1
1995	Atlanta Braves	Cleveland Indians	4-2	1968	Detroit Tigers	St. Louis Cardinals	4-3
1993	Toronto Blue Jays	Philadelphia Phillies	4-2	1967	St. Louis Cardinals	Boston Red Sox	4-3
1992	Toronto Blue Jays	Atlanta Braves	4-2	1966	Baltimore Orioles	Los Angeles Dodgers	4-0
1991	Minnesota Twins	Atlanta Braves	4-3	1965	Los Angeles Dodgers	Minnesota Twins	4-3
1990	Cincinnati Reds	Oakland Athletics	4-0	1964	St. Louis Cardinals	New York Yankees	4-3
1989	Oakland Athletics	San Francisco Giants	4-0	1963	Los Angeles Dodgers	New York Yankees	4-0
1988	Los Angeles Dodgers	Oakland Athletics	4-1	1962	New York Yankees	San Francisco Giants	4-3

* Score is represented in games played.

YEAR	WINNER	RUNNER-UP	SCORE*	YEAR	WINNER	RUNNER-UP	SCORE*
1961	New York Yankees	Cincinnati Reds	4-1	1932	New York Yankees	Chicago Cubs	4-0
1960	Pittsburgh Pirates	New York Yankees	4-3	1931	St. Louis Cardinals	Philadelphia Athletics	4-3
1959	Los Angeles Dodgers	Chicago White Sox	4-2	1930	Philadelphia Athletics	St. Louis Cardinals	4-2
1958	New York Yankees	Milwaukee Braves	4-3	1929	Philadelphia Athletics	Chicago Cubs	4-1
1957	Milwaukee Braves	New York Yankees	4-3	1928	New York Yankees	St. Louis Cardinals	4-0
1956	New York Yankees	Brooklyn Dodgers	4-3	1927	New York Yankees	Pittsburgh Pirates	4-0
1955	Brooklyn Dodgers	New York Yankees	4-3	1926	St. Louis Cardinals	New York Yankees	4-3
1954	New York Giants	Cleveland Indians	4-0	1925	Pittsburgh Pirates	Washington Senators	4-3
1953	New York Yankees	Brooklyn Dodgers	4-2	1924	Washington Senators	New York Giants	4-3
1952	New York Yankees	Brooklyn Dodgers	4-3	1923	New York Yankees	New York Giants	4-2
1951	New York Yankees	New York Giants	4-2	1922	New York Giants	New York Yankees	4-0
1950	New York Yankees	Philadelphia Phillies	4-0	1921	New York Giants	New York Yankees	5-3
1949	New York Yankees	Brooklyn Dodgers	4-1	1920	Cleveland Indians	Brooklyn Dodgers	5-2
1948	Cleveland Indians	Boston Braves	4-2	1919	Cincinnati Reds	Chicago White Sox	5-3
1947	New York Yankees	Brooklyn Dodgers	4-3	1918	Boston Red Sox	Chicago Cubs	4-2
1946	St. Louis Cardinals	Boston Red Sox	4-3	1917	Chicago White Sox	New York Giants	4-2
1945	Detroit Tigers	Chicago Cubs	4-3	1916	Boston Red Sox	Brooklyn Dodgers	4-1
1944	St. Louis Cardinals	St. Louis Browns	4-2	1915	Boston Red Sox	Philadelphia Phillies	4-1
1943	New York Yankees	St. Louis Cardinals	4-1	1914	Boston Braves	Philadelphia Athletics	4-0
1942	St. Louis Cardinals	New York Yankees	4-1	1913	Philadelphia Athletics	New York Giants	4-1
1941	New York Yankees	Brooklyn Dodgers	4-1	1912	Boston Red Sox	New York Giants	4-3
1940	Cincinnati Reds	Detroit Tigers	4-3	1911	Philadelphia Athletics	New York Giants	4-2
1939	New York Yankees	Cincinnati Reds	4-0	1910	Philadelphia Athletics	Chicago Cubs	4-1
1938	New York Yankees	Chicago Cubs	4-0	1909	Pittsburgh Pirates	Detroit Tigers	4-3
1937	New York Yankees	New York Giants	4-1	1908	Chicago Cubs	Detroit Tigers	4-1
1936	New York Yankees	New York Giants	4-2	1907	Chicago Cubs	Detroit Tigers	4-0
1935	Detroit Tigers	Chicago Cubs	4-2	1906	Chicago White Sox	Chicago Cubs	4-2
1934	St. Louis Cardinals	Detroit Tigers	4-3	1905	New York Giants	Philadelphia Athletics	4-1
1933	New York Giants	Washington Senators	4-1	1903	Boston Red Sox	Pittsburgh Pirates	5-3

Note: 1904 not played because NL-champion Giants refused to play; 1994 not played due to MLB work stoppage.

2015 DIVISION I

MEN'S BASKETBALL CHAMPIONSHIP

NATIONAL CHAMPION

COLLEGE BASKETBALL

ONE MORE FOR DUKE

After undefeated Kentucky lost in the national semi-final, the door was open for Duke to jump in and claim its fifth national champion-ship. The Blue Devils had to work hard to defeat a veteran Wisconsin team, but at the end the Devils were anything but blue.

Men's Basketball

Could Kentucky do it? That was what college hoops fans were looking for from the first tip-off of the 2014–15 season. Could the school's amazing collection of fabulous freshman run the table and become

Kentucky's Willie Cauley-Stein slams it home.

the first team since Indiana in 1976 to go undefeated? Every expert had them picked No. 1 and most figured they would win the championship.

For a very long while, it looked like those predictions would come true. Kentucky won and won and won. They did have some close calls. In January they escaped Mississippi in overtime and needed two overtimes to beat Texas A&M. They had to come from behind to beat LSU by only two points in February.

Other regular season highlights included the usual amazing upsets and rim-rattling dunks. The upsets included Michigan losing to a technical college (see page 74) and Wisconsin losing to Rutgers. Some of the surprise successes included a strong Northern Iowa team. The University of Maryland has a fine hoops tradition. But this was their first season in the powerful Big Ten. A win over Wisconsin highlighted a solid season. In the Atlantic 10, Davidson figured to be near the bottom. Wrong! They ended up winning the conference regular-season title!

In the conference tournaments, several teams put on memorable performances. In the Big 12, Iowa State was behind Texas by 10 points with a few minutes left. They went on to score the game's final 12 points and win. In the Sun Belt tournament, Georgia State came through with a last-second win. In the celebration, coach Ron Hunter tore his Achilles' tendon; he had to coach in the NCAA tournament from a rolling chair!

Meanwhile, Kentucky just kept winning. They finished the season with a loss, they romped through the SEC Tournament, winning the final over Arkansas, 78–63.

2014–2015 TOP 10
Final AP Poll

1. Duke
2. Wisconsin
3. Kentucky
4. Arizona
5. Notre Dame
6. Gonzaga
7. Michigan State
8. Virginia
9. Villanova
10. Louisville

In the NCAA tournament, with a win over Cincinnati, Kentucky did become the first team ever to reach 36–0. As expected, they reached the Final Four, but not before Notre Dame gave them a scare.

The Final Four included Kentucky, as expected, and Duke, still powerful after some mid-season losses. Wisconsin returned to the Final Four for the second straight year, led by **Frank "The Tank" Kaminsky** (see box). Michigan State was the surprise entry. Seeded No. 7, the Spartans knocked off several higher-ranked teams on their way to Indianapolis. The season did not end as the experts had predicted after all! Read our full NCAA tournament coverage starting on page 76.

FRANK THE TANK!

Wisconsin superstar **Frank Kaminsky** could have skipped his senior season and headed right to the riches of the NBA. He would have been a very high draft pick for sure. But he had been disappointed with how his junior season ended, with a loss in the NCAA semifinals. He wanted another shot at the championship. He almost made it. Kaminsky returned and led Wisconsin one step farther, but not to the top. Still, he brought home an impressive set of trophies. Kaminsky was the clear winner of just about every player of the year award. He won the Wooden Award, the Naismith Award, the AP Player of the Year Award, and the Oscar Robertson Trophy. Though he leaves college without the one trophy he really wanted, he can look back with pride on a great run with the Badgers.

2015 ALL-AMERICAS

Willie CAULEY-STEIN, F	Kentucky
Jerian GRANT, G	Notre Dame
Frank KAMINSKY, F	Wisconsin
Jahlil OKAFOR, C	Duke
D'Angelo RUSSELL, G	Ohio State

Hoop Highlights

The ball bounced up and down a lot this year . . . it always does. Here are some of the most memorable bounces of the 2014–15 men's NCAA season.

Father Knows Best

To open the season, No. 8 Louisville took on Minnesota. No big deal, right? Wrong. Louisville's coach is the legendary **Rick Pitino**. Minnesota is led by **Richard Pitino**–Rick's son. It was the first time they had coached against each other. Dad showed that he had the edge on Son after Louisville won 81–68. But Rick was not happy and said after the game, "I hate the fact that we won. I'd rather have not played it, because my son lost."

Answered Prayer

Long-range buzzer-beaters are part of basketball, but this was ridiculous. After Manhattan missed a free throw but still led by one point, **Jalen Jenkins** of George Mason got the rebound. He took a dribble and then launched the ball from the free-throw line . . . toward the other end of the court. After soaring 75 feet, his shot went in and George Mason was the winner.

◀◀◀ Now That's a Hot Hand

Florida State was battling state rival Miami and trailed late in the game in February. That's when freshman **Xavier Rathan-Mayes** took over. He became a one-man team and scored an amazing 30 points in just over four-and-a-half minutes! He had only five points in the game before he began this streak and was averaging only 13 points a game heading into the contest. Unfortunately, his teammates were not so hot and Miami ended up winning anyway, 81–77.

Ultimate Upset

Michigan was ranked No. 17, is a member of the mighty Big Ten, and has a history of success. The New Jersey Institute of Technology didn't even have a conference and had recently suffered through a 51-game losing streak. But

◀◀◀ **At the Buzzer**

Albany was expected to return to the NCAA tournament, but they needed a miracle in the America East championship game. **Peter Hooley** grabbed a loose rebound and heaved up a three-point shot that won the championship at the buzzer over Stony Brook. Clutch!

the records didn't matter. NJIT buried three after three while Michigan was ice cold. Still, the game was close. Two free throws with 4.5 second left gave NJIT its final two-point lead and they held one for the shocking win.

Ultimate Upset II

The Connecticut Huskies were the NCAA champs last year. Yale didn't even make the NCAA tournament. The two teams met in December and it looked like the roles were reversed. Yale outrebounded UConn on offense, 13–1, and built a 12-point lead. UConn came back, though, and led by one with 1.7 seconds left. Though Yale's **Jack Montague** had not made a bucket all game, he picked the right time to bury a three that gave Yale a stunning 45–44 win.

A Grand Day

On January 25, Duke coach **Mike Krzyzewski** (let's just say "Coach K") earned his 1,000th win leading the Blue Devils. He is the first men's hoops coach to reach that level at any NCAA division.

Thanks, Coach

Duke and North Carolina are two of the biggest rivals in college hoops. At their February game in 2014, however, they put that aside before the game to honor former UNC coach **Dean Smith**, who had died a few days before. Both teams gathered at midcourt for a moment of silence. The silence turned to cheers as both teams played what some called the best game of the year. Duke won a thriller that went to overtime, 92–90.

23.1

Congratulations to **Tyler Harvey** of Eastern Washington. He led the nation in scoring with that points-per-game average. The bad news? That was the lowest top average since 1949! Experts around the country are worried that college hoops is becoming too slow and too slow-scoring. Teams averaged about 68 points a game, the lowest since the 1950s.

NCAA Tournament

First and Second Round Highlights

Fab First Four! The tournament includes 68 teams, with a special First Four playoff to determine who will be part of the 64-team field. One of 2015's First Four games was epic. In a rare high-scoring battle, Mississippi overcame a hot-shooting BYU team, 92–90. BYU was actually ahead by 17 at halftime. A 62-point second-half by Mississippi turned that around and then BYU missed a three-point late that could have given the Cougars the game.

Rebounding Rules! UAB cleaned the glass so well over Iowa State, they ended up chasing the No. 3 seed back home. UAB was only a No. 14 seed, but they beat the Big Twelve champs 60–59 in the tournament's first big upset.

◀◀◀**Panthers Can Beat Bears!** That headline might not work in nature, but it worked in basketball. No. 14 seed Georgia State pulled off the biggest upset of the first round by beating No. 3 Baylor. Georgia State won 57–56 by scoring the last 13 points of the game to stage a remarkable comeback. The game-winning points came on a three-pointer by R. J. Hunter. Seconds later, Hunter had to help his dad and coach Ron up from the floor. The injured coach had fallen off his rolling chair as he celebrated his son's big shot!

Take That, Experts! When the 64-team field was announced, several experts were shocked that UCLA had been chosen from the Pac-12. The Bruins had won 22 games, but were apparently not good enough for the experts. Those guys were all proven wrong as No. 11 seed UCLA upset No. 6 SMU in the first round, 60–59. They got their final points on a goaltending call on a three-point basket. UCLA rubbed it in, too. They beat UAB to become the lowest-seeded team to make the Sweet 16.

Second Round Surprise! The only No. 1 team not to make the Final Four was Villanova. The reason was their second-round upset at the hands of No. 8 seed North Carolina State. Pressure D by the Wolfpack held the Wildcats to only 31 percent shooting. Meanwhile, four NC State players reached double digits in scoring and their team danced into the Sweet 16 with a 71–68 win.

Tom Terrific Been there, done that. Michigan State was seeded No. 7, facing No. 2 Virginia. In 2014, the Spartans sent the Cavaliers home . . . and they repeated the feat this year! The win was nothing new for MSU coach Tom Izzo. He ran his record in the round of 32 teams to 13–1!

Close, But Not Quite A trio of lower-seeded teams gave a couple of top schools all they could handle. Northeastern was making its first appearance in 20 years and nearly defeated No. 4 Notre Dame. UC Irvine was the surprise Big West entry. They were driving for a winning or tying basket when a last-second turnover ended their upset hopes over Louisville. And if Valparaiso had made a last-second three-pointer, it would have ended Maryland's streak of tournament-opening wins at 10, but the Terrapins held on.

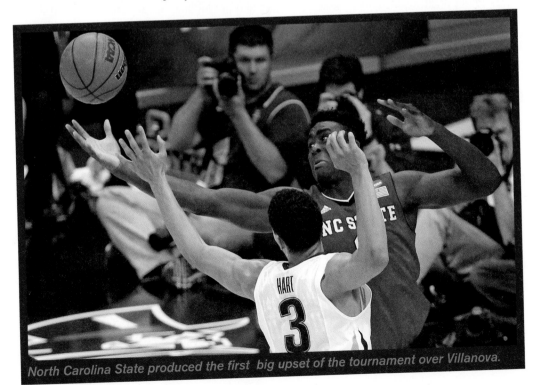

North Carolina State produced the first big upset of the tournament over Villanova.

NCAA Tournament

Regional Finals Highlights

▶ On their way to the Final Four, Kentucky squashed West Virginia, beating them by the playground-like score of 78–39.

▶ Kentucky had its toughest test of the season in the Elite Eight. Notre Dame led by six with about six minutes left, but the Wildcats stormed back. They made their last nine shots of the game and won 68–66.

▶ Louisville ended North Carolina State's upset run, before being upset itself by Michigan State, which had upset No. 3 seed Oklahoma already.

▶ The Pac-12 sent two teams into the Elite Eight: Arizona and Utah. Both lost, however, when they faced Final Four teams in Wisconsin and Duke.

Kaminsky (44) was clutch for the Badgers.

a flow. It was a great back-and-forth game, and was tied at halftime, 36–36. Wisconsin scored nine straight points early in the second half, but Kentucky came back to lead by four ten minutes later. The end game was the key. Kentucky went cold, and the Badgers got hot. They were nearly perfect on free throws and kept the pressure on Kentucky to respond. Moments later, Wisconsin was on the way to the title game.

National Semifinals

Wisconsin 71–Kentucky 64

Take down that 0, Kentucky. Wisconsin did what 38 other teams had tried and failed to do. They beat unbeaten Kentucky thanks to a solid offense and a defense that never let the Wildcats get into

Duke 81–Michigan State 61

The Spartans' surprising run ended with a clear win by Duke. MSU had no answer for Duke's Jahlil Okafor, who had 18 points, or Justise Winslow, who had 19. In a season in which he won his 1,000th game, Duke's Coach K was aiming to move into second place all-time for NCAA titles.

IT'S DUKE!

2015 NCAA CHAMPIONSHIP

Add 2015 to a list that includes 1991, 1992, 2001, and 2010. That makes five NCAA men's basketball champions for Duke University . . . all under the leadership of Coach **Mike Krzyzewski**. His five titles are now the second most all-time behind the probably-untouchable record of 10 by UCLA's **John Wooden**.

The game that gave Coach K his fifth was a great battle, with multiple lead changes. Things could have gone either way until Duke closed it out late in the game.

Led by national player of the year **Frank Kaminsky**, Wisconsin came out strong. They grabbed an early lead and let Duke know this would not be easy. By halftime, the game was tied 36–36. The second half started out all Badgers, as they built a nine-point lead. Duke stormed back with an 11–3 run and were behind by only a point midway through the half. And they did all that with star **Jahlil Okafor** in foul trouble that kept him on the bench for far fewer than his usual minutes.

In the game's final five minutes, Duke put its foot on the gas. Freshman sensation **Tyus Jones** made a three-pointer to put Duke up by eight. Duke scored ten straight points that sealed the game. Wisconsin did get it down to three points, but Duke's offense never let the Badgers get closer.

The Blue Devils held on and a disappointed Wisconsin finished out of the money again; they lost in the semifinals last year. The final was 68–63 . . . and five.

Most Outstanding Player

Duke freshman guard **Tyus Jones** led all scorers in the title game with 23 points and didn't miss a free throw. He was named the Most Outstanding Player of the Final Four.

All-Time NCAA Titles

NO.	SCHOOL
11	UCLA
7	Kentucky
5	Duke
	Indiana
	North Carolina
3	Kansas
	Connecticut

Coach K knows to pack scissors at the Final Four.

Women's Basketball

SEASON HIGHLIGHTS

▶ A double-double in hoops is reaching double digits in two stat categories. Oral Roberts forward **Vicky McIntyre** reeled off 27 of those games this season, including 14 straight at one point! She ended up leading the NCAA in rebounding with 15.8 per game.

▶ Congrats to **Kelsey Mitchell** of Ohio State for a nation-leading 24.9 points per game average.

▶ Mount Saint Joseph player **Lauren Hill** inspired millions by making just 10 points. Why such a big deal? She was dying from

Vicky McIntyre (34) was double-trouble!

a brain tumor, but battled back to be able to play briefly. Her good cheer and courage earned national praise. Sadly, Lauren passed away in April.

▶ Connecticut coach **Geno Auriemma** reached his 900th career victory with a win over Cincinnati in February. He is the sixth coach of a women's team to reach that mark.

▶ Did UConn ever lose? Well . . . once. The Huskies came into 2014 without having lost in a year. On November 17, however, No. 6–ranked Stanford battled UConn until the last second, and emerged with an 88–86 win. (Of course, Stanford lost to unranked Arizona in February . . . one of only 10 Arizona wins!)

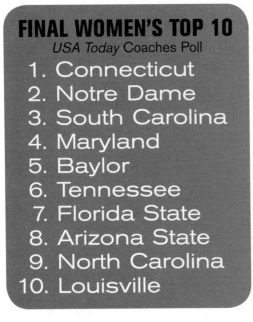

FINAL WOMEN'S TOP 10
USA Today Coaches Poll

1. Connecticut
2. Notre Dame
3. South Carolina
4. Maryland
5. Baylor
6. Tennessee
7. Florida State
8. Arizona State
9. North Carolina
10. Louisville

NCAA CHAMPIONSHIP

SEMIFINAL 1

In one of the best games of the season, Notre Dame held off a very strong South Carolina team by one point to earn a return trip to the national championship game. The game was a defensive battle, as South Carolina tried to slow the fast-moving Fighting Irish attack. It almost worked. South Carolina trailed by as many as a dozen, but fought back to take the lead with about a minute left. Notre Dame retook a one-point lead when **Madison Cable** made her only basket of the game. South Carolina had time for one more shot . . . but missed. Notre Dame would face Connecticut again after the 66–65 squeaker.

SEMIFINAL 2

Maryland might have thought it was in good shape, riding a 28-game winning streak. That streak and any good feelings ended soon in their semifinal against Connecticut. The Huskies dominated, swooping in for rebounds and blocking shots left and right. The final was 81–58, but it wasn't that close!

NATIONAL CHAMPIONSHIP GAME

The Connecticut Huskies captured their third straight championship by defeating Notre Dame, 63–53. Coach **Geno Auriemma** tied the great John Wooden on the men's side with his tenth career title.

Notre Dame was good, that's for sure. But Connecticut was just overpowering. They won two of their first three games in the NCAA tournament by more than 50 points. So when Notre Dame kept the margin down to 10 . . .

Three for three: Breanna Stewart (30) was the MOP.

that was almost like a win! In fact, it was just the second time since UConn's second-game loss to Stanford way back in November that any team had been within 15 points of the Huskies at the end.

Breanna Stewart earned her third straight Most Outstanding Player award, even though she scored only 8 points in the final. Pulling down 15 rebounds to lead both teams was what earned her many of the votes.

How good was UConn? They led the nation in scoring offense (89.3 points per game) *and* scoring defense (allowing only 48.6 ppg). Wow. In the past three seasons, their record is an amazing 113-5. Double wow. Their three straight championships tie the record . . . which they first tied in 2004!

NCAA Champs!

MEN'S DIVISION I

Open with Duke in 2015—close with Duke, here in 2010.

2015 **Duke**	2004 **Connecticut**	1993 **North Carolina**
2014 **Connecticut**	2003 **Syracuse**	1992 **Duke**
2013 **Louisville**	2002 **Maryland**	1991 **Duke**
2012 **Kentucky**	2001 **Duke**	1990 **UNLV**
2011 **Connecticut**	2000 **Michigan State**	1989 **Michigan**
2010 **Duke**	1999 **Connecticut**	1988 **Kansas**
2009 **North Carolina**	1998 **Kentucky**	1987 **Indiana**
2008 **Kansas**	1997 **Arizona**	1986 **Louisville**
2007 **Florida**	1996 **Kentucky**	1985 **Villanova**
2006 **Florida**	1995 **UCLA**	1984 **Georgetown**
2005 **North Carolina**	1994 **Arkansas**	1983 **NC State**
		1982 **North Carolina**
		1981 **Indiana**
		1980 **Louisville**
		1979 **Michigan State**
		1978 **Kentucky**
		1977 **Marquette**
		1976 **Indiana**
		1975 **UCLA**
		1974 **NC State**
		1973 **UCLA**

1972 **UCLA**	1948 **Kentucky**	1943 **Wyoming**
1971 **UCLA**	1947 **Holy Cross**	1942 **Stanford**
1970 **UCLA**	1946 **Oklahoma A&M**	1941 **Wisconsin**
1969 **UCLA**	1945 **Oklahoma A&M**	1940 **Indiana**
1968 **UCLA**	1944 **Utah**	1939 **Oregon**
1967 **UCLA**		
1966 **Texas Western**		

WOMEN'S DIVISION I

1965 **UCLA**	2015 **Connecticut**	1998 **Tennessee**
1964 **UCLA**	2014 **Connecticut**	1997 **Tennessee**
1963 **Loyola (Illinois)**	2013 **Connecticut**	1996 **Tennessee**
1962 **Cincinnati**	2012 **Baylor**	1995 **Connecticut**
1961 **Cincinnati**	2011 **Texas A&M**	1994 **North Carolina**
1960 **Ohio State**	2010 **Connecticut**	1993 **Texas Tech**
1959 **California**	2009 **Connecticut**	1992 **Stanford**
1958 **Kentucky**	2008 **Tennessee**	1991 **Tennessee**
1957 **North Carolina**	2007 **Tennessee**	1990 **Stanford**
1956 **San Francisco**	2006 **Maryland**	1989 **Tennessee**
1955 **San Francisco**	2005 **Baylor**	1988 **Louisiana Tech**
1954 **La Salle**	2004 **Connecticut**	1987 **Tennessee**
1953 **Indiana**	2003 **Connecticut**	1986 **Texas**
1952 **Kansas**	2002 **Connecticut**	1985 **Old Dominion**
1951 **Kentucky**	2001 **Notre Dame**	1984 **USC**
1950 **City Coll. of N.Y.**	2000 **Connecticut**	1983 **USC**
1949 **Kentucky**	1999 **Purdue**	1982 **Louisiana Tech**

GOLD FOR GOLDEN STATE!
The backcourt duo of Klay Thompson and Stephen Curry were all smiles as they held the Larry O'Brien Trophy after winning the Warriors' first NBA championship since 1975. All they had to do was beat LeBron!

New Teams on Top

The Hawks flew, the Warriors battled, the Rockets soared, and the Cavaliers . . . did whatever cavaliers do. A new crop of NBA teams rose to the top of the heap in 2014–15, while some traditional powerhouses suffered big letdowns.

Atlanta's surprise success led the news for most of the season. Atlanta won only 38 games in 2013–14, but improved by 22 this season. The team did not boast any superstars, but instead played a tight-passing game that got everyone involved. Their amazing run in January almost guaranteed them a playoff spot (see page 92).

In the West, Golden State was a team on the rise, but few expected so much so soon. They were led by the backcourt duo of **Stephen Curry** and **Klay Thompson**. Curry's excellent three-point shooting opened up the court, while Thompson also displayed great skills from the outside. The Warriors had the best overall record in the NBA and set a team record with 67 wins.

James Harden has long been one of the NBA's top players, but this season, he took his stardom to new heights. He led the Rockets to their first playoff series win in six years and finished second in MVP voting while scoring more points (2,217) than any other player.

In Cleveland, **LeBron James** picked up the Cavaliers and carried them into the NBA Finals. In his first season back in his hometown—and with the team he started his pro career with—James helped the Cavs improve by 20 wins.

The Boston Celtics made news, too, as they won 40 games and made the playoffs with a completely new roster.

STAR BROS! The NBA All-Star Game in February featured a sports first. **Marc Gasol** of the Memphis Grizzlies and **Pau Gasol** of the Chicago Bulls were elected by fans to start the All-Star Game. They became the first brothers ever to start the mid-season event. Growing up in Spain, the pair probably never imagined that they'd face off in the contest. Thanks to a win by younger brother Marc's West team, he'll have bragging rights in the Gasol house . . . until next game!

Coach Hammon?

Becky Hammon was one of the top players in the WNBA for 16 seasons. The seven-time All-Star retired after the 2014 season as one of the all-time leaders in assists. She has taken her game to another court, though. The San Antonio Spurs named her as the second woman ever to work as an assistant coach for the men's top league.

On the other side of the win-loss battle, some famous NBA teams had terrible seasons. The Los Angeles Lakers have won the second-most NBA titles ever, but in 2014–15 they set a team record with 61 losses. That is not a record any team wants to set! With star **Kobe Bryant** often injured, the Lakers struggled throughout the season. On the other coast, one of the oldest NBA teams, the New York Knicks, also set a team record with 65 losses. Not even re-signing star shooter **Carmelo Anthony** was enough to save the Knickerbockers. Also, two-time NBA champ Miami suffered after James left them for Cleveland. After making the NBA Finals in 2014, they didn't even make the playoffs.

The ball bounces up and down . . . so do the fortunes of NBA teams. Read on to see who ended up bouncing the highest!

2014–2015 FINAL STANDINGS

EASTERN CONFERENCE

ATLANTIC DIVISION	W–L
Raptors	49-33
Celtics	40-42
Nets	38-44
76ers	18-64
Knicks	17-65

CENTRAL DIVISION	W–L
Cavaliers	53-29
Bulls	50-32
Bucks	41-41
Pacers	38-44
Pistons	32-50

SOUTHEAST DIVISION	W–L
Hawks	60-22
Wizards	46-36
Heat	37-45
Hornets	33-49
Magic	25-57

WESTERN CONFERENCE

NORTHWEST DIVISION	W–L
Trail Blazers	51-31
Thunder	45-37
Jazz	38-44
Nuggets	30-52
Timberwolves	16-66

PACIFIC DIVISION	W–L
Warriors	67-15
Clippers	56-26
Suns	39-43
Kings	29-53
Lakers	21-61

SOUTHWEST DIVISION	W–L
Rockets	56-26
Grizzlies	55-27
Spurs	55-27
Mavericks	50-32
Pelicans	45-37

2015 Basketball Playoffs

Chris Paul looped in this shot to beat the Spurs.

FIRST ROUND HIGHLIGHTS

➤ The defending champion San Antonio Spurs fell to the L.A. Clippers after a classic Game 7. L.A. guard **Chris Paul** battled a leg injury to score 27 points. The last two came on a wild, last-second bank shot that thrilled the home fans.

➤ The Atlanta Hawks kept their amazing season going by knocking off the Brooklyn Nets, wrapping it up in six games with a 111–87 pasting.

➤ **James Harden** led the Houston Rockets to a five-game win over the Dallas Mavericks, the first playoff series win for Houston since 2009.

➤ The Memphis Grizzlies, led by **Marc Gasol**'s 26 points and 14 rebounds in Game 5, stopped the Portland Trail Blazers from advancing.

SEMIFINALS

➤ The Hawks kept flying, beating a young and talented Washington Wizards squad.

➤ Chicago's playoff dreams ended by order of the King, **LeBron James**, whose Cavaliers beat the Bulls in six games.

➤ The NBA's top team showed why they got there in the regular season. Golden State sent Memphis home in six games, with MVP **Stephen Curry** leading the way.

➤ One of the biggest shockers of the entire playoffs: L.A. led Houston three games to one, but the Rockets stormed back to win three straight and knock out the Clippers. **James Harden** poured in 31 points in a solid Game 7 win.

CONFERENCE FINALS

➤ Atlanta finally met a team it couldn't beat. After a dominating regular season and a smooth playoff run, the Hawks finally landed. James and the Cavaliers put together four outstanding games and swept Atlanta. Game 3 went to overtime, but otherwise, Cleveland had their way.

➤ Golden State punched its golden ticket to the NBA Finals for the first time in 40 years. The Warriors beat Houston in five games.

2015 Basketball Finals

GAME 1
Warriors 108, Cavs 100
Cleveland closed the gap late to force overtime, thanks largely to **LeBron James's** 44 points. In overtime, though, they went cold. Golden State's **Stephen Curry** buried four free throws, while James missed his first three shots.

GAME 2
Cavs 95, Warriors 93
For the first time ever, the first two NBA Finals games went to overtime. James had a triple-double (39 points, 16 rebounds, 11 assists), while Aussie super-sub **Matthew Dellavedova** buried clutch free throws in overtime.

GAME 3
Cavs 96, Warriors 91
James poured in another 40 points and Delly scored a surprising 20 filling in for **Kyrie Irving**. Curry found his shooting touch, pouring in 17 points in a fourth-quarter binge, but it was not enough to stop Cleveland from taking a 2-1 series lead.

GAME 4
Warriors 103, Cavs 82
This game will be remembered for the TV closeups of James's head. He crashed into a camera at courtside and gashed his scalp. He scored his series-low 20 points. Golden State also got a big contribution from forward **David Lee**, who came off the bench to spark the team. A solid team effort tied the series.

GAME 5
Warriors 104, Cavs 91
Not even another triple-double by James could stop the Warriors. Curry pumped in 37 points in a back-and-forth game that included 20 lead changes. Inspired by their home crowd, the Warriors pulled ahead.

GAME 6
Warriors 105, Cavs 97
Golden State won its first NBA championship since 1975. Finals MVP **Andre Iguodala** scored 25 key points and play tough D. Even forward **Draymond Green** got into the act with a triple-double, while Curry had 25 points. The Warriors from the Golden State took home the golden trophy!

Curry showed he can score from inside, too.

Basketball Awards

MVP FOR THREE

Points, that is. **Stephen Curry** was clearly the best player in the NBA, leading the Warriors to their best record ever and then on to the NBA title. Curry broke his own single-season record for three-point field goals with 286. In the playoffs, he poured in another 98, setting another record. He also led the league in free-throw percentage at 91.4 percent. He follows in the footsteps of his dad, **Dell**, who was also a great long-range shooter in 16 NBA seasons.

NBA AWARDS

SIXTH MAN	**Lou Williams,** Raptors
MOST IMPROVED	**Jimmy Butler,** Bulls
TOP DEFENDER	**Kawhi Leonard,** Spurs
ROOKIE OF THE YEAR	**Andrew Wiggins,** Timberwolves
ALL-STAR GAME MVP	**Russell Westbrook,** Thunder
COACH OF THE YEAR	**Mike Budenholzer,** Hawks

Basketball Stat Leaders

Most NBA stats are ranked "per game" (pg). That is, the numbers below represent the average each player had for all his games in 2014–15.

28.1 POINTS (PPG)
Russell Westbrook, Thunder

10.2 ASSISTS (APG)
Chris Paul, Clippers

15.0 REBOUNDS (RPG)
DeAndre Jordan, Clippers

5.3 OFF. REBOUNDS (ORPG)
Andre Drummond, Pistons

2.3 STEALS (SPG)
Kawhi Leonard, Spurs

2.9 BLOCKS (BPG)
Anthony Davis, Pelicans

71.0 FG PCT.
DeAndre Jordan, Clippers

91.4 FT PCT.
Stephen Curry, Warriors

2,217

That's how many points **James Harden** of the Rockets scored to lead the NBA. He didn't win the scoring title, however, as his per-game average was just below Russell Westbrook's.

In the Paint

Year of the Dribble

In honor of the Bay Area's many Chinese-American residents, Golden State put on special uniforms in February. The design was for the Chinese New Year in February. The red-and-yellow coloring is for good luck; the Chinese characters translate to "year of the goat," which is what most of 2015 will be.

◀◀◀ Move Over, Michael

The Lakers had one of their most forgettable seasons ever, setting a team record for lowest winning percentage (.256). Perhaps the only bright spot came in December, when star guard **Kobe Bryant** passed the great **Michael Jordan** on the all-time scoring list. Bryant went past Jordan's 32,292 and ended the season third all-time with 32,482 points.

Quick Shot

What can you do in 0.2 seconds? Not much. But **Trevor Booker** can score in an NBA

A MAGIC MONTH

In January 2015, everything went right for the Atlanta Hawks. And we mean everything! The high-flying Eastern Conference leaders became the first team to go 17-0 for a month. As a result, Atlanta got another special honor. The entire starting five—**Paul Millsap**, **Jeff Teague**, **Kyle Korver**, **Al Horford**, and **DeMarre Carroll**—were named the collective NBA Player of the Month. Showing how much the team shares its success, each of those five averaged double figures in scoring in January.

Who Was That Masked Man?

In February and March, Oklahoma City's **Russell Westbrook** went on a serious tear. In an eight-game span, he had six triple-doubles, including four in a row. Amazingly, he missed one game in that stretch after suffering a broken bone in his cheek. After sitting for a day, he returned to his triple-double streak, this time wearing a protective plastic mask. He scored 40 points before the mask . . . and 49 the first day he wore it! Westbrook went on to lead the NBA in scoring.

game. The Utah Jazz forward had that much time on the shot clock when the ball was in-bounded to him. He tapped it backward over his head like a volleyball player . . . and the ball went in before the buzzer!

Coach Dad?

Austin Rivers could not call up Dad to complain about his coach. That's because when Austin was traded to the L.A. Clippers in January, his new coach *was* his dad! **Doc Rivers** welcomed Austin as a backup point guard who helped the team reach the Western Conference semifinals.

Titanic Thompson

An NBA player putting in 37 points has had a great night shooting. What do you call a player who pours in that many . . . in a 12-minute quarter?! Golden State's **Klay Thompson** was more than just the go-to guy in the third quarter against Sacramento in January. He was unstoppable. Thompson's NBA single-quarter record total included another record 9 three-pointers as part of perfect 13-for-13 quarter. Toss in two free throws

and you get 37. "As many spectacular things as **Michael [Jordan]** did, which he did nightly, I never saw him do that," said an amazed Warriors coach **Steve Kerr**.

> **❝ My dad would never, ever play me over somebody because I'm his son. If I'm not playing well, I'm sitting on the bench.❞**
>
> **— AUSTIN RIVERS** ON PLAYING FOR HIS DAD, DOC

Not Appreciated

Most teams hold a Fan Appreciation Night to thank their loyal supporters. The teams give gifts or have special awards. Orlando's fans are probably wondering about the Magic's 2015 celebration. The Magic and the visiting Knicks only scored 15 points in the entire second quarter. It was the fewest points in a quarter since the NBA started using the 24-second shot clock way back in 1954! The teams made a combined 6 of 43 shots and had nine turnovers. Yuck!

2014 WNBA

Maya Moore was magic in Minnesota.

The Phoenix team in the WNBA takes its name from the stuff that tells the temperature in thermometers: mercury. In 2014, the temperature for the Phoenix Mercury read HOT! They won an all-time WNBA record 29 games, capping it off with a powerful sweep in the WNBA Finals (page 95) to win their third title in eight seasons.

"They are definitely in the discussion as one of the best [teams] of all time," former WNBA star **Rebecca Lobo** said on WNBA.com.

The Mercury were led by center **Brittney Griner** and guard **Diana Taurasi**. Griner set a new WNBA record with 129 blocks and was the defensive player of the year.

The Mercury didn't have the best player, however. Minnesota star **Maya Moore**, who led the Lynx to the title in 2013, earned her first MVP award. She averaged 23.9 points per game to lead the league.

The Western Conference championship series between those two teams was basically the WNBA championship. While the Mercury and the Lynx dominated the West, the East was not as strong. Only the Atlanta Dream finished with a winning record. The Chicago Sky came from fourth place in the East to earn a spot in the finals.

With stars like Griner and Moore, and growing attendance in several league cities, the future of the WNBA looks almost as hot as the Mercury's play on the court!

2014 AWARDS AND LEADERS

MVP: Maya Moore, Minnesota Lynx

ROOKIE OF THE YEAR: Chiney Ogwumike, Connecticut Sun

DEFENSIVE PLAYER OF THE YEAR: Brittney Griner, Phoenix Mercury

SCORING: Maya Moore, Minnesota Lynx, 23.9 ppg

REBOUNDS: Courtney Paris, Tulsa Shock, 10.2 rpg

ASSISTS: Diana Taurasi, Phoenix Mercury, 5.6 apg

Courtney Vandersloot, Chicago Sky, 5.6 apg

2014 WNBA FINALS

GAME 1: Mercury 83, Sky 62

When you've got a 6'8" center on your side, good things happen. Phoenix defensive star **Brittney Griner** set a WNBA playoff record with 8 blocks as the Mercury took Game 1. **Candice Dupree** led all scorers with 26 points, while **Diana Taurasi** chipped in 19. Dupree didn't miss in the first half, and the Mercury set another record with a 22-point halftime lead. A back injury kept Sky star **Elena Delle Donne** from playing much.

GAME 2: Mercury 97, Sky 68

The Sky tried to chop down the tall tree that is **Griner**. She got scratched in the eye and cracked a tooth, but she kept battling. Griner led her team to another dominating win. Even with **Delle Donne** coming back to score 22 points, it was not enough. A 15–2 run by Phoenix in the second quarter sealed the Sky's fate. The 29-point victory margin was the biggest in WNBA Finals history.

GAME 3: Mercury 87, Sky 82

Griner's eye injury kept her from the court, but the Mercury were so deep, it didn't matter. They celebrated afterward as Phoenix won its third WNBA championship, 87–82. The absence of the big star made the game closer. But an equally big star came through.

58.5

That was the WNBA Finals record shooting percentage for the Mercury in their Game 1 romp.

Taurasi, the Finals MVP, scored 14 of her 24 points in the fourth quarter. None were bigger than the last jumper she made with 14.3 seconds. That shot (followed by some free throws) clinched the win and the trophy.

Griner and Taurasi: Phoenix's titanic twosome.

Stat Stuff

NBA CHAMPIONS

2014-15 **Golden State**	2000-01 **L.A. Lakers**	1986-87 **L.A. Lakers**
2013-14 **San Antonio**	1999-00 **L.A. Lakers**	1985-86 **Boston**
2012-13 **Miami**	1998-99 **San Antonio**	1984-85 **L.A. Lakers**
2011-12 **Miami**	1997-98 **Chicago**	1983-84 **Boston**
2010-11 **Dallas**	1996-97 **Chicago**	1982-83 **Philadelphia**
2009-10 **L.A. Lakers**	1995-96 **Chicago**	1981-82 **L.A. Lakers**
2008-09 **L.A. Lakers**	1994-95 **Houston**	1980-81 **Boston**
2007-08 **Boston**	1993-94 **Houston**	1979-80 **L.A. Lakers**
2006-07 **San Antonio**	1992-93 **Chicago**	1978-79 **Seattle**
2005-06 **Miami**	1991-92 **Chicago**	1977-78 **Washington**
2004-05 **San Antonio**	1990-91 **Chicago**	1976-77 **Portland**
2003-04 **Detroit**	1989-90 **Detroit**	1975-76 **Boston**
2002-03 **San Antonio**	1988-89 **Detroit**	1974-75 **Golden State**
2001-02 **L.A. Lakers**	1987-88 **L.A. Lakers**	1973-74 **Boston**

1972-73 **New York**	1956-57 **Boston**	1950-51 **Rochester**
1971-72 **L.A. Lakers**	1955-56 **Philadelphia**	1949-50 **Minneapolis**
1970-71 **Milwaukee**	1954-55 **Syracuse**	1948-49 **Minneapolis**
1969-70 **New York**	1953-54 **Minneapolis**	1947-48 **Baltimore**
1968-69 **Boston**	1952-53 **Minneapolis**	1946-47 **Philadelphia**
1967-68 **Boston**	1951-52 **Minneapolis**	

WNBA CHAMPIONS

1966-67 **Philadelphia**	2014 **Phoenix**	2005 **Sacramento**
1965-66 **Boston**	2013 **Minnesota**	2004 **Seattle**
1964-65 **Boston**	2012 **Indiana**	2003 **Detroit**
1963-64 **Boston**	2011 **Minnesota**	2002 **Los Angeles**
1962-63 **Boston**	2010 **Seattle**	2001 **Los Angeles**
1961-62 **Boston**	2009 **Phoenix**	2000 **Houston**
1960-61 **Boston**	2008 **Detroit**	1999 **Houston**
1959-60 **Boston**	2007 **Phoenix**	1998 **Houston**
1958-59 **Boston**	2006 **Detroit**	1997 **Houston**
1957-58 **St. Louis**		

NHL

THREE FOR STANLEY
Chicago Blackhawks players crowd around the Stanley Cup, which they won for the third time in six seasons by defeating the Tampa Bay Lightning in six games.

2014-2015 Season

When the NHL season began, many fans looked for the previous season's finalists to return to the Stanley Cup Finals. However, for the first time since 2006—and only the fifth time ever—the champion did not return to the postseason. The Los Angeles Kings finished fourth in their division and did not earn a playoff spot.

The Kings were not the only team from the West to lose a crown. The Colorado Avalanche acted like their name and plummeted down the standings mountain. In 2014, they led the Central Division. In 2015, they finished last. The San Jose Sharks missed the playoffs for the first time since 2003.

Another top team had a down year in 2015. The Boston Bruins had the most points in the NHL in 2013–14, but also missed the 2015 playoffs.

Of course, with so many top teams falling back, other teams had a chance to rise. The Winnipeg Jets made the biggest move, going from last place in the Central Division to their first playoff spot since 2007 (when they were the Atlanta Thrashers). The Nashville Predators also jumped into the playoff hunt, scoring 104 points.

One team that has been more successful than any in NHL history had one of its best seasons ever. The Montreal Canadiens have won 23 Stanley Cups, far more than any other team. In 2014–15, they racked up the most points since 1989, leading the Atlantic Division. Their key player was the outstanding goalie **Carey Price**. How dominant was he? Price became the first player since fellow Canadien **José Théodore** to be named both top goalie and NHL MVP (see page 106).

Amid the elevator rides up and down the standings, a few teams continued to play very well. The New York Rangers were Stanley Cup finalists last

Carey Price

Winnipeg fans got their playoff wish.

season, and then put up the highest point total in the NHL in 2014–15. The Chicago Blackhawks won the Cup in 2010 and 2013 and were ready to make a trio of Stanleys. They boasted a strong defense that gave up 189 goals, tied for fewest in the league with the Price-led Canadiens.

Meanwhile, the Tampa Bay Lightning were the NHL's highest-scoring team, leading the way with 262 goals thanks to sharpshooters like **Steven Stamkos** and **Tyler Johnson**.

In the end, the new teams to the playoffs didn't last long and the survivors in the Final were only a little surprising. Read all about the playoffs starting on page 102.

GOODBYE...HELLO

The New York Islanders have played in Nassau County, New York, on Long Island since 1972. The Islanders won four Stanley Cups there (1980–83) and fans have many great memories. Beginning in the 2015–16 season, their home will be Brooklyn, New York. They'll play in the Barclays Center that is also home to the Brooklyn Nets NBA team.

The NHL also announced that it was looking into adding teams in the near future. One possibility: Las Vegas!

FINAL STANDINGS

EASTERN CONFERENCE

ATLANTIC DIVISION	PTS	METROPOLITAN DIVISION	PTS
1. Montreal*	110	1. NY Rangers*	113
2. Tampa Bay*	108	2. Washington*	101
3. Detroit*	100	3. NY Islanders*	101
4. Ottawa*	99	4. Pittsburgh*	98
5. Boston	96	5. Columbus	89
6. Florida	91	6. Philadelphia	84
7. Toronto	68	7. New Jersey	78
8. Buffalo	54	8. Carolina	71

WESTERN CONFERENCE

CENTRAL DIVISION	PTS	PACIFIC DIVISION	PTS
1. St. Louis*	109	1. Anaheim*	109
2. Nashville*	104	2. Vancouver*	101
3. Chicago*	102	3. Calgary*	97
4. Minnesota*	100	4. Los Angeles	95
5. Winnipeg*	99	5. San Jose	89
6. Dallas	92	6. Edmonton	62
7. Colorado	90	7. Arizona	56

*Made NHL playoffs

Stanley Cup Playoffs

Here are some highlights (or lowlights, depending on what team you root for) from the 2015 Stanley Cup playoffs:

◎ The Islanders said goodbye to their old home (page 101) with a playoff game win on April 25, but lost the series to Washington.

◎ The Minnesota Wild pulled the biggest upset of the first round, beating No.1 seed St. Louis in six games.

◀◀◀ In Game 4 of the Blackhawks-Predators series, there was an unusual timeout. After making a save, Predators goalie **Pekka Rinne** couldn't find the puck. It had slipped inside his pads during the play. It took him, his teammates, and the referees more than three minutes to dig in there and find it. Things got worse when Chicago won that game in triple overtime.

◎ The Winnipeg Jets' Cinderella run to the playoffs ended quickly. The mighty Anaheim Ducks swept the Jets in four games.

◎ The Lightning struck like their name at the end of Game 3 against the Canadiens. Tampa Bay's **Tyler Johnson** scored with just 1.1 seconds left to break a 1–1 tie and win the game.

Back-to-Back Comebacks

In Games 4 and 5 of the Western Conference Finals, both the Chicago Blackhawks and Anaheim Ducks made furious comebacks, only to see the opponent win in overtime. In Game 4, the Ducks trailed 3–1 in the third period. Then the Ducks quacked and fast, scoring three goals in 37 seconds to take the lead. But Chicago scored to tie it and then won in ovetime. It was déjà vu in Game 5 . . . in reverse. Chicago trailed by two goals with under two minutes to play. But Chicago's **Jonathan Toews** scored twice to tie the game. Anaheim then won in overtime, but the comeback energized Chicago, which went on to win the series.

Stanley Cup Finals

Tampa Bay and Chicago faced off in what became an entertaining, closely fought Stanley Cup Final. The first five games were each decided by one goal, which hadn't happened since 1951! In the end, Chicago's defense was too much for the high-scoring Tampa Bay team, and the Blackhawks kissed their third Stanley Cup in six seasons.

GAME 1 Third-period goals from **Teuvo Teräväinen** and **Antoine Vermette** gave Chicago a win on the road. They shut out the Lightning for the final 55 minutes.

GAME 2 A third-period power-play goal by Tampa Bay's **Jason Garrison** evened the series. Tampa Bay scored three of the game's final four goals.

GAME 3 The game was a 1–1 defensive struggle until the third period. Chicago took the lead, but **Ondřej Palát** and **Cedric Paquette** scored to give the Lightning the series lead.

GAME 4 More late-game magic from Chicago, as **Brandon Saad** scored late in the third period to thrill Chicago's hometown fans.

GAME 5 This was another nail-biter, with both goalies showing off impressive saves. **Vermette** got his second goal of the series at just the right time, with two minutes left in the game.

GAME 6 Chicago goalie **Corey Crawford** had 25 saves and made his teammates' two goals stand up to record the first shutout of the series. **Patrick Kane's** third-period goal iced the championship for Chicago.

Chicago's Marián Hossa

Hockey Highlights

O Canada!

Winnipeg hosted a playoff game for the first time in 19 years. It was a great year for Canadian NHL fans, as five of the seven teams from the Great White North made the postseason.

Will This Game Ever End?

When regular-season games end in a tie, the NHL plays a five-minute overtime period. If there is still no winner, the teams have a shootout: one skater vs. the goalie. In a December 2014 game, the Washington Capitals and Florida Panthers, it took an NHL record 20 rounds to determine the winner. Florida won on **Nick Bjugstad's** goal past a tired Capitals keeper.

Perfect Timing!

The race for the NHL scoring title went down to the final minutes of the season. Entering the Dallas Stars' last game, **Jamie Benn** was a point behind **John Tavares** of the Islanders. Tavares got two more points to end with a season total of 86. But Benn got a hat trick (three goals) and an assist to end with 87 points. The four-point finale was part of a three-game 10-point streak, so Benn finished with a flourish!

The McDavid Sweepstakes

Every once in a while, a young player comes along who everyone agrees will be a superstar. The Great One, **Wayne Gretzky**, was a player like that. In the NBA, it was **LeBron James**. In baseball, **Mike Trout** was a young phenom. In 2015, **Connor McDavid**, a junior player from Ontario, was that young star. NHL teams seemed like they were trying to lose to get the chance to draft him No. 1 in the NHL Draft. The Edmonton Oilers ended up winning the NHL Draft Lottery . . . and choosing the league's best new player.

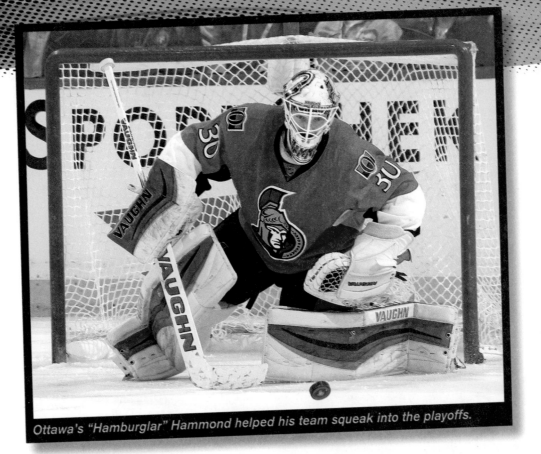

Ottawa's "Hamburglar" Hammond helped his team squeak into the playoffs.

He'll Never Go Hungry

Andrew Hammond made the most of his chance as Ottawa's goalie. He took over in February and did his best brick wall imitation. Hammond won 14 of his first 16 games in net. What made him really famous was his nickname, "Hamburglar" Hammond. In fact, McDonald's gave him a card that lets him have free food there . . . for life!

Mumps? Really?

Mumps is a disease that usually affects very young people. It infects glands and causes fever and headaches. People with mumps often have very swollen faces. It is highly contagious. In late 2014, more than a dozen NHL players came down with the disease, including Penguins star Sidney Crosby. They all got better, but it was a weird thing to see on the NHL injury report.

Up the Charts

Jaromír Jágr, now a forward with Florida, has been skating in the NHL for 21 seasons, longer than some of his young teammates have been alive! In 2015, the 43-year-old Jágr moved up to fifth on the all-time list for goals; he ended the season with 722. He also is now sixth on the assists list with 1,080. And yes, he expects to be back in uniform in 2015–16!

2014-15 Awards

Hart Trophy (MVP),
Vezina Trophy (Best Goaltender),
Ted Lindsay Award
(Top player as chosen by players)
CAREY PRICE, Montreal

Norris Trophy (Best Defenseman)
ERIK KARLSSON, Ottawa

"I'd really like to encourage First Nations youth to be proud of your heritage and don't be discouraged from the improbable. Sunachailya!"

— **CAREY PRICE**, AFTER WINNING MVP (HE SAID THANKS IN THE LANGUAGE SPOKEN BY HIS ULKATCHO PEOPLE. IN CANADA, NATIVE PEOPLE ARE CALLED PART OF THE FIRST NATIONS.)

Conn Smythe Trophy
(Stanley Cup Playoffs MVP)
DUNCAN KEITH, Chicago

Art Ross Trophy (Top Scorer)
JAMIE BENN, Dallas

Calder Memorial Trophy (Top Rookie)
AARON EKBLAD, Florida

Frank Selke Trophy
(Best Defensive Forward)
PATRICE BERGERON, Boston

Lady Byng Memorial Trophy
(Most Gentlemanly Player)
◀◀◀**JIŘÍ HUDLER,** Calgary

Jack Adams Award (Best Coach)
BOB HARTLEY, Calgary

Masterton Award (Sportsmanship)
DEVAN DUBNYK, Minnesota

Mark Messier Award (Leadership)
JONATHAN TOEWS, Chicago

2014–15 Stat Leaders

87 POINTS
Jamie Benn, Dallas ▶▶▶

53 GOALS
Alex Ovechkin, Washington

60 ASSISTS
Nicklas Backstrom, Washington

1.96 GOALS AGAINST AVG.
.933 SAVE PERCENTAGE
44 WINS
Carey Price, Montreal

1,175 FACEOFFS WON
Patrice Bergeron, Boston

+38 PLUS/MINUS
Max Pacioretty, Montreal
Nikita Kucherov, Tampa Bay

238 PENALTY MINUTES
Steve Downie, Pittsburgh

24

The Detroit Red Wings have made the NHL Playoffs for that many years in a row. That's far and away the most in the NHL, but also the longest among any team in the NFL, NBA, or MLB.

Stanley Cup Champions

2014–15	**Chicago Blackhawks**	1988–89	**Calgary Flames**
2013–14	**Los Angeles Kings**	1987–88	**Edmonton Oilers**
2012–13	**Chicago Blackhawks**	1986–87	**Edmonton Oilers**
2011–12	**Los Angeles Kings**	1985–86	**Montreal Canadiens**
2010–11	**Boston Bruins**	1984–85	**Edmonton Oilers**
2009–10	**Chicago Blackhawks**	1983–84	**Edmonton Oilers**
2008–09	**Pittsburgh Penguins**	1982–83	**New York Islanders**
2007–08	**Detroit Red Wings**	1981–82	**New York Islanders**
2006–07	**Anaheim Ducks**	1980–81	**New York Islanders**
2005–06	**Carolina Hurricanes**	1979–80	**New York Islanders**
2004–05	No champion (Lockout)	1978–79	**Montreal Canadiens**
2003–04	**Tampa Bay Lightning**	1977–78	**Montreal Canadiens**
2002–03	**New Jersey Devils**	1976–77	**Montreal Canadiens**
2001–02	**Detroit Red Wings**	1975–76	**Montreal Canadiens**
2000–01	**Colorado Avalanche**	1974–75	**Philadelphia Flyers**
1999–00	**New Jersey Devils**	1973–74	**Philadelphia Flyers**
1998–99	**Dallas Stars**	1972–73	**Montreal Canadiens**
1997–98	**Detroit Red Wings**	1971–72	**Boston Bruins**
1996–97	**Detroit Red Wings**	1970–71	**Montreal Canadiens**
1995–96	**Colorado Avalanche**	1969–70	**Boston Bruins**
1994–95	**New Jersey Devils**	1968–69	**Montreal Canadiens**
1993–94	**New York Rangers**	1967–68	**Montreal Canadiens**
1992–93	**Montreal Canadiens**	1966–67	**Toronto Maple Leafs**
1991–92	**Pittsburgh Penguins**	1965–66	**Montreal Canadiens**
1990–91	**Pittsburgh Penguins**	1964–65	**Montreal Canadiens**
1989–90	**Edmonton Oilers**	1963–64	**Toronto Maple Leafs**

1962–63	Toronto Maple Leafs
1961–62	Toronto Maple Leafs
1960–61	Chicago Blackhawks
1959–60	Montreal Canadiens
1958–59	Montreal Canadiens
1957–58	Montreal Canadiens
1956–57	Montreal Canadiens
1955–56	Montreal Canadiens
1954–55	Detroit Red Wings
1953–54	Detroit Red Wings
1952–53	Montreal Canadiens
1951–52	Detroit Red Wings
1950–51	Toronto Maple Leafs
1949–50	Detroit Red Wings
1948–49	Toronto Maple Leafs
1947–48	Toronto Maple Leafs
1946–47	Toronto Maple Leafs
1945–46	Montreal Canadiens
1944–45	Toronto Maple Leafs
1943–44	Montreal Canadiens
1942–43	Detroit Red Wings
1941–42	Toronto Maple Leafs
1940–41	Boston Bruins
1939–40	New York Rangers
1938–39	Boston Bruins
1937–38	Chicago Blackhawks
1936–37	Detroit Red Wings
1935–36	Detroit Red Wings
1934–35	Montreal Maroons

MOST STANLEY CUP TITLES

Montreal Canadiens	23
Toronto Maple Leafs	13
Detroit Red Wings	11
Boston Bruins	6
Chicago Blackhawks	6

1933–34	Chicago Blackhawks
1932–33	New York Rangers
1931–32	Toronto Maple Leafs
1930–31	Montreal Canadiens
1929–30	Montreal Canadiens
1928–29	Boston Bruins
1927–28	New York Rangers
1926–27	Ottawa Senators
1925–26	Montreal Maroons
1924–25	Montreal Canadiens
1923–24	Montreal Canadiens
1922–23	Ottawa Senators
1921–22	Toronto St. Patricks
1920–21	Ottawa Senators
1919–20	Ottawa Senators
1918–19	Montreal Canadiens
1917–18	Toronto Arenas

CHAMPIONS!

With a dominating 5–2 win over Japan in the Women's World Cup final, the United States took home their longed-for trophy. They also got revenge against Japan, who had beaten them in the 2011 final. The win kicked off a week of celebrations for a group of winners—and friends.

SOCCER

Great Soccer!

Colombia "headed off" France at the pass!

The 2015 team was expected to carry on in that winning tradition and was ranked No. 1 in the world heading into the World Cup, which was played in cities throughout Canada. The U.S. team that would try to win a third Cup for America included veterans like all-time leading scorer **Abby Wambach** and midfielder **Carli Lloyd** and newcomers including midfielder **Morgan Brian** and defenders **Julie Johnston** and **Meghan Klingenberg**. Together, they created memories to last a lifetime in one of the best performances by an American sports team ever. But before they could lift the trophy, they had a gauntlet of games to run. Eight groups of four teams battled for a spot in the 16-team "knockout" round.

Opening Round Highlights

HOME COOKING: The World Cup was held in cities all over Canada. The host nation gave its fans a nice treat by beating China, 1–0, in the tournament opener.

BIG NUMBERS: Germany is one of the world's best teams. Côte d'Ivoire is, um . . . not. Germany dominated, winning 10–0. Switzerland matched that with a 10–1 win over Ecuador.

BIG UPSET: The biggest upset of the first round came when Colombia knocked off France, 2–0. Goalie **Sandra Sepulveda** was outstanding, while her team's offense

The highlight of the past year's sports season was different for every fan, but for millions of people around the world, it was the Women's World Cup of soccer.

As it has been since the first World Cup back in 1991, the American team was in the spotlight. Since winning that first Cup, the US team has always been one of the world's best, adding a second title in 1999. They were the runners-up in 2011, too.

was very aggressive, giving France more than it could handle.

AFRICAN STARS: In its first Women's World Cup, Cameroon made it to the round of 16 by upsetting Switzerland, 2–1. Their dream ended in a tough 1–0 loss to China.

SAD "TRI": Mexican soccer teams are called "El Tri" after the nation's three-color flag. But as hard as they tried, the women's team could not perform well at this World Cup. They tied Colombia, but lost their other two matches, including 5–0 to France.

26.7

That's the number in millions of people who watched the US-Japan Women's World Cup final. That was the largest audience EVER for a US soccer match, men's or women's.

AMERICA'S FIRST THREE

* The Americans got off to a sluggish start, but rallied to win their first game, 3-1 over Australia. **Megan Rapinoe** scored two solid goals. **Christen Press** scored as well.

* Just because there are no goals does not mean it wasn't a great game. Sweden almost pulled off a big upset, but US goalie **Hope Solo** was awesome. The game ended in a 0-0.

* **Abby Wambach** has scored more goals than any woman in US history. She added another on a great header for the only score to beat Nigeria, 1-0.

Abby Wambach scored a key goal for the US in the opening round.

Women's World Cup Playoffs

Knockout Round

In soccer, they call the playoffs the "knockout" round. That's when teams that lose are knocked out of the event. The US team faced three very tough opponents but came out on top to make it back to the final. First, they defeated Colombia, 2–0, in the round of 16. Then it was on to the quarterfinals.

Angerer saved Germany with a penalty-kick save.

Quarterfinals

→ **USA 1, China 0: Hope Solo** put up another shutout in goal. Captain **Carli Lloyd** banged in a header in the 53rd minute. That was enough to hold off a talented team from China.

→ **Germany 1, France 1:** After 120 minutes, the score was still tied, so these two teams went to penalty kicks. German keeper **Nadine Angerer** stopped the final French kick and Germany advanced.

→ **Japan 1, Australia 0:** The Aussies' great run ended as Japan used its speed and ball control to keep the team from Down Under scoreless.

→ **England 2, Canada 1:** The home team couldn't fight past the best English team in years.

Semifinals

→ **USA 2, Germany 0:** The US dodged a bullet when Golden Boot winner **Celia Sasic** missed a penalty kick. Lloyd made hers and **Kelley O'Hara** added a clincher late in the game. The US headed to the World Cup final for the second time in a row.

→ **Japan 2, England 1:** A shocking ending sent England home in tears. With just minutes left in the game, England knocked in an own goal on a deflection to give Japan a spot in the final.

Women's World Cup
Champions!

This shot by Lloyd started at midfield for her third goal.

Tobin Heath (center) capped off the Americans' amazing victory.

Rarely has a major championship been won so quickly and so decisively. US captain **Carli Lloyd** slipped home a goal on a corner kick about three minutes into the Women's World Cup final against Japan. Just two minutes later, she found the ball in a scramble off another corner kick. In the 14th minute, **Lauren Holiday** slammed in a volley for the third goal.

And just two minutes after that, the goal of the tournament gave Lloyd a hat trick. After collecting a loose ball, she looked up and saw the Japanese goalie off her line. Lloyd cracked a shot that traveled more than 50 yards in the air. The goalie got a finger on it, but could not stop it from hitting the net.

With just about 15 percent of the game over . . . it was basically over. Japan could not respond to the American onslaught. They did break the Americans' long streak of not allowing a goal when **Yuki Ogimi** scored in the 27th minute. At 540 minutes, the streak tied for the longest in WWC history.

In the second half, American defender **Juli Johnston** scored an own goal, but **Tobin Heath** capped off the scoring a few minutes later to make the final result 5–2.

Veterans **Abby Wambach** and **Christie Rampone** hoisted the trophy, the third Women's World Cup for the US, the most all-time. They won the first event in 1991 and also won in 1999.

GOLDEN BALL (MVP)
Carli Lloyd, USA

GOLDEN BOOT
(TOP SCORER)
Celia Sasic, Germany

GOLDEN GLOVE
(TOP GOALIE)
Hope Solo, USA

TOP YOUNG PLAYER
Kadeisha Buchanan, Canada

2014 MLS Cup

Captain Keane's overtime goal was the winner.

The Galaxy actually made the 2014 MLS Cup after losing to Seattle in a playoff game. However, MLS plays a two-game, total-goals semifinal, and the teams each scored two goals. A goal by LA in the game in Seattle earned them the tiebreaker on "away" goals. They faced the New England Revolution in the MLS Cup.

Once the Galaxy made it there, they made the most of it. **Gyasi Zardes** scored in the second half for a 1–0 lead. Zardes is easily spotted by his hairdo, dyed bright blond. He says that he does that so his grandmother can find him when she watches TV! New England tied it later on a **Chris Tierney** goal.

It was on to overtime!

The teams appeared headed to penalty kicks until the league MVP decided things. **Robbie Keane** had 19 goals for the Galaxy in 2014, but none bigger than his 111th-minute game-winner. The Galaxy's win was a perfect sendoff for captain **Landon Donovan** (see box), who retired after the game.

The Los Angeles Galaxy are the most successful team ever in Major League Soccer. In 2014, they won their fifth MLS Cup—most all-time in the 19-year-old league—and third in four seasons. A galaxy of stars is a big reason, and they keep adding to their collection of top players and titles.

Good-bye, Landon!

Landon Donovan said good-bye to soccer after the greatest career in US history. He played in three World Cups, scoring five goals in those games. He is the nation's all-time leader with 57 international goals. Fifteen of his goals came on penalty kicks—on 15 tries! His 2010 game-winner against Algeria in the World Cup was called the second-biggest goal in US history by *Sports Illustrated*. In Major League Soccer, he was also dominant. Playing most of his career with the LA Galaxy, Donovan won six MLS titles (he won his first two with San Jose) and is the league's all-time leading scorer with 144. He'll be missed, but never forgotten.

Premier League

New TV deals are sending English soccer's Barclays Premier League to America more than ever. US fans responded by picking their favorites and getting up Saturday morning to watch great soccer . . . or should we say "football"?

Pro soccer has been played in England since 1888, but the Premier League started in 1992. It is the top rank of England's multi-level pro system. One of the coolest things about this system is called relegation. That is, after each season, the bottom three teams from each level move down. The top three teams move up. Imagine if baseball's Boston Red Sox had a terrible 2015 season (they did!) and had to move down to play Triple A (they didn't!).

Chelsea's Eden Hazard help the Blues win the EPL.

The Premier League doesn't have a playoff system, either. They play 38 games from August to May, usually two a week. Teams get three points for a win and one point for a tie. The team with the most points win the league.

In 2015, FC Chelsea won the title easily, with 87 points, eight ahead of runner-up Manchester City. It was Chelsea's first title in five seasons, but it has been among the top teams for a while, winning four titles in all since 2004. That's a big turaround for a club that had not finished on top in the 50 seasons before that!

Don't feel sorry for runners-up. The top four teams earn a spot in the UEFA Champions League, the most important international club tournament (see page 118). Check out some Premier League games on American TV!

2015 Championships

Messi brought another trophy to Barcelona.

that scored the most goals in the other team's home stadium wins (see box).

A team that wins its league, then a league cup (a knockout tournament in its country), and then the Champions League is a rare thing. It's called winning the "treble" (owning three titles at once). By defeating Italian club Juventus, 3–1, FC Barcelona became the first team to capture the treble . . . twice! It was their fifth Champions League title ever as well.

Barcelona is like an all-star team. It includes scoring wizards **Lionel Messi**, **Neymar**, and **Luis Suárez**, along with a defensive wall that includes Spanish World Cup winners **Gerard Piqué** and **Sergio Busquets**.

In the final, Suarez scored the game-winner after the game was tied 1–1. Neymar capped it off by scoring with the final kick of the game.

Champions League

Winning your soccer league in Europe is a great accomplishment, but that's not enough for the top teams. Top clubs earn a spot in the following year's UEFA Champions League, a series that attracts some of the biggest TV audiences of the year.

Except for the one-game final, the knockout rounds are played in two games each. The team that scores the most goals in both games wins. If there's a tie, the team

Quarterfinals

▶ **Bayern Munich 7**, FC Porto 4

▶ **FC Barcelona 5**, Paris St. Germain 1

▶ **Juventus 1**, FC Monaco 0

▶ **Real Madrid 1**, Atlético Madrid 0

Semifinals

▶ **FC Barcelona 5**, Bayern Munich 3

▶ **Juventus 3**, Real Madrid 2

NOTE: Scores are two-game total goals.

Gold Cup

The Gold Cup is played among teams that are part of CONCACAF. That's the name of the region that includes North and Central America and the Caribbean. The United States and Mexico have dominated the event, which began in 1991. Mexico had captured six titles, while the US was the defending champ, having won in 2013.

Mexico struggled through qualifying matches, however, and needed controversial penalty-kick calls to advance to the final.

Playing in front of home fans (the 2015 Gold Cup was played in several US cities), the United States made it to the semifinals, where they were shocked by Jamaica. That Caribbean country had only beaten the US once in 22 tries and the US was a heavy favorite. Jamaica won 2–1 and made its first Gold Cup final.

Order was restored in the final, however. Mexico played well and won easily, 3–1.

Copa America

The biggest soccer tournament in South America—other than the World Cup every four years—is the Copa America. National teams from around the continent, along with a few guests, play for the championship. The 2015 Copa was played in Chile and the host nation took home the top prize.

Many fans around the world hoped that this might be the year that Argentina's magical star, **Lionel Messi**, would finally get a trophy for playing for his country. He has won many league cups with FC Barcelona, but nothing of importance for Argentina.

But not even Messi's magic could crack the Chilean wall. However, Chile could not score either, even in the extra time. The game went to penalty kicks and Messi's teammates let him down. He was the only Argentine to make his kick. Chile won its first-ever Copa America as the home fans rejoiced.

Surrounded by their home fans, Chile celebrated its first Copa America title.

Stat Stuff

MAJOR LEAGUE SOCCER
CHAMPIONS

2014	Los Angeles Galaxy
2013	Sporting Kansas City
2012	Los Angeles Galaxy
2011	Los Angeles Galaxy
2010	Colorado Rapids
2009	Real Salt Lake
2008	Columbus Crew
2007	Houston Dynamo
2006	Houston Dynamo
2005	Los Angeles Galaxy
2004	D.C. United
2003	San Jose Earthquakes
2002	Los Angeles Galaxy
2001	San Jose Earthquakes
2000	Kansas City Wizards
1999	D.C. United
1998	Chicago Fire
1997	D.C. United
1996	D.C. United

World Cup Scoring Leaders

MEN

GOALS	PLAYER, COUNTRY
16	Miroslav Klose, Germany
15	Ronaldo, Brazil
14	Gerd Müller, West Germany
13	Just Fontaine, France
12	Pelé, Brazil
11	Jürgen Klinsmann, Germany
11	Sandor Kocsis, Hungary

WOMEN

GOALS	PLAYER, COUNTRY
15	Marta, Brazil
14	Abby Wambach, USA
14	Birgit Prinz, Germany
12	Michelle Akers, USA
11	Bettina Wiegmann, Germany
11	Sun Wen, China

WOMEN'S WORLD CUP

YEAR	CHAMPION	RUNNER-UP
2015	**United States**	Japan
2011	**Japan**	United States
2007	**Germany**	Brazil
2003	**Germany**	Sweden
1999	**United States**	China
1995	**Norway**	Germany
1991	**United States**	Norway

UEFA CHAMPIONS LEAGUE

The Champions League pits the best against the best. The top club teams from the members of UEFA (Union of European Football Associations) face off in a months-long tournament. They squeeze the games in among their regular league games, so the winners need to be talented and extremely fit. Read about the 2015 winner on page 118. Here are other recent Champions League champions!

2015 FC Barcelona/SPAIN
2014 Real Madrid/SPAIN
2013 Bayern Munich/GERMANY
2012 Chelsea FC/ENGLAND
2011 FC Barcelona/SPAIN
2010 Inter (Milan)/ITALY
2009 FC Barcelona/SPAIN
2008 Manchester United/ENGLAND

2007 AC Milan/ITALY
2006 FC Barcelona/SPAIN
2005 Liverpool FC/ENGLAND
2004 FC Porto/PORTUGAL
2003 AC Milan/ITALY
2002 Real Madrid/SPAIN
2001 Bayern Munich/GERMANY

HEADING HOME AT HOMESTEAD
The 2014 NASCAR Chase for the Sprint Cup ended at Homestead- Miami Speedway in Florida with Kevin Harvick as the champion. He finished ahead of three other final challengers to capture his first overall series championship.

NASCAR

NASCAR 2014

The 2014 NASCAR season had a new flavor . . . and it tasted like winning. NASCAR organizers created a new way for drivers to make it into the season-ending Chase for the Sprint Cup. With a couple of exceptions, the rule was "you win . . . you're in." That meant that winning one race in an otherwise down year could earn a driver a spot in the racing playoffs.

Plus, during the final 10-race Chase, drivers were eliminated after every few races (see box). The original field of 16 was cut down to a "final four" for the last race of the year at Homestead in Florida. In that race, whichever of the four finalists finished highest would be the champion. It turned out that NASCAR got more than it bargained for, as the chase-within-the-Chase was hot, heated, and hairy! Then, the final race (page 127) turned into one of the most thrilling of the year.

The 2014 season began with a real treat for longtime NASCAR fans. **Dale Earnhardt Jr.**, a regular winner of the most popular driver award, thrilled his fans by winning the season-opening Daytona 500. "Winning this race is the greatest feeling you can feel in the sport, aside from accepting the trophy for the championship," Earnhardt said.

Then, as the season raced ahead, each winner joined Earnhardt in the Chase. No one really leaped out as a top contender, and it was not until **Kevin Harvick** won at Darlington that there was a repeat winner.

Six-time NASCAR champ and 2013 winner **Jimmie Johnson** leaped into the Chase with a stunning string of successes in late spring, winning three of four races.

There's nothing like winning your first NASCAR Sprint Cup race, as Aric Almirola did in July.

CHASE FOR THE CUP

2014 FINAL STANDINGS

1. **Kevin HARVICK**
2. **Ryan NEWMAN**
3. **Denny HAMLIN**
4. **Joey LOGANO**
5. **Brad KESELOWSKI**
6. **Jeff GORDON**
7. **Matt KENSETH**
8. **Dale EARNHARDT, Jr.**
9. **Carl EDWARDS**
10. **Kyle BUSCH**
11. **Jimmie JOHNSON**
12. **Kurt BUSCH**

Kasey Kahne slipped in with a win in Atlanta.

Aric Almirola was another surprise, winning the July race at Daytona, his first ever as a Sprint Cup driver. It was not the first for his car number, however. Almirola was driving the famous No. 43 car once steered by the legendary Richard Petty, who won a record 200 races and a record-tying seven NASCAR titles. A.J. Allmendinger won his first Sprint Cup race ever at Watkins Glen to earn his first spot in the Chase. Kasey Kahne was the last driver to qualify with a win at Atlanta just before the Chase began.

On the outside looking in—without a chance to claim a season title—were such big names as Tony Stewart, Danica Patrick, and Jamie McMurray.

When the dust settled, 13 drivers had won races and earned their spot in the Chase. Three others slid in at the back of the pack based on points earned throughout the season.

And so, the Chase was on!

HOW THEY CHASED

Here's how the 10-race Chase for the Cup was organized, round by round.

Challenger Round: Chicago, New Hampshire, Dover (Delaware)

The bottom four of the 16 drivers were eliminated after these races.

Contender Round: Kansas, Charlotte, and Talladega

The bottom four of the 12 remaining drivers were cut.

Eliminator Round: Martinsville (Virginia), Texas, and Phoenix

It started with eight drivers and ended with the top four still rolling.

Sprint Cup Championship: Homestead, Florida

The highest finisher among the final four drivers in this race wins the Cup.

The Chase

Logano got the Chase off to a roaring start with wins in New Hampshire and Kansas.

The Challenger Round

Brad Keselowski started the Chase with the most wins by any driver. He won the Chase-opening race at *CHICAGO*, rallying from a 25th-place starting position. That put him into the next round, and put pressure on the other 15 drivers. Joey Logano earned the win in *NEW HAMPSHIRE*. Jeff Gordon earned his 92nd career win in *DOVER* to stay in the hunt.

The Contender Round

Logano added a second victory in *KANSAS* to clinch a spot in the final eight, as Keselowski and others had tire trouble that sent them falling in the standings. Kevin Harvick won in *CHARLOTTE* the following week to join Logano in the next round. Following the race, Matt Kenseth and Keselowski got into a fistfight in the garage area, with both crews racing to break up the squabble. Keselowski was fined heavily. The pressure of the Chase was building. At famous *TALLADEGA*, Keselowski was on the bubble, needing a win to stay in the Chase. He came through in a final-lap sprint to outpace Jimmie Johnson and Dale Earnhardt Jr., among others.

The Eliminator Round

A big win by fan favorite Earnhardt at MARTINSVILLE kept his slim hopes alive. In TEXAS, six-time champion Johnson won the race, but it was a hollow victory. He had been eliminated from the Chase after the previous round. Gordon bumped with Keselowski and ended up with a flat tire . . . and in 29th. He went from the top of the points to near the bottom.

His season in jeopardy, the four-time champ was angry and confronted Keselowski on pit road after the race. In PHOENIX, in the last race before the final, the drama was up front. Harvick put on a dominating performance to earn a spot in the final four Chase drivers. Behind him, however, Ryan Newman was crawling through the remaining cars. He needed to finish eleventh to get the points he needed to race for the title in Miami. With a final-lap pass, he did it! In the process, he knocked Jeff Gordon from a chance at a fifth title.

The Championship: HOMESTEAD!

Kevin Harvick, **Ryan Newman**, **Joey Logano**, and **Denny Hamlin** were the survivors of the the exciting Chase for the Cup in 2014. They all arrived in Miami as the only drivers who could win the season title . . . whoever finished highest in the final race took home the top prize.

NASCAR fans got all that they wanted, as all those drivers except Logano were neck-and-neck with less than 10 laps to go.

After a restart, Hamlin sprinted to the lead. Another caution flag slowed the field, and this time Harvick, sporting four fresh tires, moved up even farther on the restart. After a final restart, Harvick blew past Hamlin and then held Newman off to finish ahead of all three other drivers. Harvick earned his first NASCAR Sprint Cup season championship.

Harvick's nickname is "Happy." In 2014, he got a new one: "Champion."

Around the Track

⏫ The Road Killers

A.J. Allmendinger earned the first Cup win of his career in dramatic fashion as he held off **Marcos Ambrose** in the final laps at Watkins Glen. Both drivers are outstanding road racers, expert at the twists and turns of Watkins, one of two road courses on the NASCAR season. This race was close throughout, with each driver taking turns in the lead. Allmendinger held off Ambrose through three late restarts before winning the green-white-checkered sprint to the finish line.

Remember to Lock Your Car!

It's hard to drive in a NASCAR race without a car, but that's what **Travis Kvapil** had to deal with after his was stolen from a hotel parking lot! Kvapil had to miss the race in Atlanta after his No. 44 car, its trailer, and the truck pulling the trailer disappeared. Kvapil asked the public for help on Twitter: "Wow. Anyone near Atlanta find my stolen Cup car let me know! Unreal." The car was found unharmed the next day, but not in time for the race.

7 ➔ 0

Race drivers usually aim for going from zero to really fast. **Matt Kenseth** went the other way in 2014. He won a career-best seven races in 2013 . . . and then put up a bagel in 2014!

The Kid Wins!

In September 2014, when most of his friends were in school, **Cole Custer** was busy winning a race. The 16-year-old held off eventual series champion **Matt Crafton** to become the youngest person ever to win a NASCAR race. Cole won the UNOH 175 in the Camping World Truck Series. "I've been coming to these races since I was really young," he said. "I've looked up to this series and everyone that has raced in this series. I could never imagine being here racing and winning. I can't even explain how amazing this feels."

Well, Finally

Jimmie Johnson has won six NASCAR championships and 74 career races. He has won on short tracks, medium tracks, and long tracks . . . down South, out West, and in the Northeast. But until 2014, he had never won at the Michigan International Speedway. Something always seemed to go wrong when he and his team went there. But the 24-race Michigan losing streak stopped when he grabbed a late lead and never gave it up. "We had figured out every way to lose this race," Johnson said. "And today we were able to get it done."

◀◀◀Power in the Poconos

Dale Earnhardt Jr. won the Pocono 400 in 2014, driving for Hendrick Motorsports. But that was nothing new: Hendrick seems to own the track, site of two NASCAR races each season. Earnhardt's win was the fifth in a row since 2012 for Hendrick.

2014: **Dale Earnhardt Jr.** (twice)

2013: **Jimmie Johnson** and **Kasey Kahne**

2012: **Jeff Gordon**

Other NASCAR News

Nationwide Series

This is the training ground for future Sprint Cup champs, and **Chase Elliott** made a good name for himself in 2014. The son of former NASCAR champ **"Million Dollar Bill" Elliott**, Chase won three races and ended up atop the Xfinity points standings. The second rank of NASCAR racing will run under the Xfinity brand starting in 2015. The name changed, but the hard-charging racing continued, as drivers tried to win races as well as attract attention from Sprint Cup team owners.

ONE TO WATCH

Kyle Larson was the NASCAR Rookie of the Year in 2014. Larson finished second in two Chase for the Cup and was the top non-Chase driver in the standings. He showed that he truly belonged among the big boys. He started out 2015 with five top 10s in his first 13 races, too.

1997
NASCAR WINSTON CUP C

Jeff Gordon's Last Season

In early 2015, the great **Jeff Gordon** announced that he was racing his final season in NASCAR. Gordon came from Indiana to take NASCAR by storm, winning his first season championship in 1995, when he was just 24 years old. He won again in 1997 (pictured), 1998, and 2001. His four titles are third most behind **Richard Petty**, **Dale Earnhardt Sr.** (7 each), and **Jimmie Johnson** (6). Gordon had 92 wins entering the 2015 season and had won at least one race each season except two from 1994–2014. He'll go down as one of the all-time greats in motor sports.

SPLISH, SPLASH!

NASCAR vehicles don't come with windshield wipers . . . but for the first part of the 2015 season, they would have come in handy. Five of the first 15 races were hit by rain at some point. The Michigan race didn't even finish all its laps. The delays took some of the drama out of the days for fans and drivers, but you can't outrace Mother Nature!

Camping World Truck Series

Matt Crafton didn't win the most races in the 2014 truck racing campaign . . . but he was steady enough that his 833 points were enough to nip runner-up **Ryan Blaney** for the title. Winning was nothing new for Matt, however. Crafton became the first driver to win consecutive championships in the Camping World Truck Series.

NASCAR Champions

YEAR	DRIVER	CAR MAKER	YEAR	DRIVER	CAR MAKER
2014	Kevin Harvick	Chevrolet	1994	Dale Earnhardt Sr.	Chevrolet
2013	Jimmie Johnson	Chevrolet	1993	Dale Earnhardt Sr.	Chevrolet
2012	Brad Keselowski	Dodge	1992	Alan Kulwicki	Ford
2011	Tony Stewart	Chevrolet	1991	Dale Earnhardt Sr.	Chevrolet
2010	Jimmie Johnson	Chevrolet	1990	Dale Earnhardt Sr.	Chevrolet
2009	Jimmie Johnson	Chevrolet	1989	Rusty Wallace	Pontiac
2008	Jimmie Johnson	Chevrolet	1988	Bill Elliott	Ford
2007	Jimmie Johnson	Chevrolet	1987	Dale Earnhardt Sr.	Chevrolet
2006	Jimmie Johnson	Chevrolet	1986	Dale Earnhardt Sr.	Chevrolet
2005	Tony Stewart	Chevrolet	1985	Darrell Waltrip	Chevrolet
2004	Kurt Busch	Ford	1984	Terry Labonte	Chevrolet
2003	Matt Kenseth	Ford	1983	Bobby Allison	Buick
2002	Tony Stewart	Pontiac	1982	Darrell Waltrip	Buick
2001	Jeff Gordon	Chevrolet	1981	Darrell Waltrip	Buick
2000	Bobby Labonte	Pontiac	1980	Dale Earnhardt Sr.	Chevrolet
1999	Dale Jarrett	Ford	1979	Richard Petty	Chevrolet
1998	Jeff Gordon	Chevrolet	1978	Cale Yarborough	Oldsmobile
1997	Jeff Gordon	Chevrolet	1977	Cale Yarborough	Chevrolet
1996	Terry Labonte	Chevrolet	1976	Cale Yarborough	Chevrolet
1995	Jeff Gordon	Chevrolet	1975	Richard Petty	Dodge

YEAR	DRIVER	CAR MAKER	YEAR	DRIVER	CAR MAKER
1974	Richard Petty	Dodge	1961	Ned Jarrett	Chevrolet
1973	Benny Parsons	Chevrolet	1960	Rex White	Chevrolet
1972	Richard Petty	Plymouth	1959	Lee Petty	Plymouth
1971	Richard Petty	Plymouth	1958	Lee Petty	Oldsmobile
1970	Bobby Isaac	Dodge	1957	Buck Baker	Chevrolet
1969	David Pearson	Ford	1956	Buck Baker	Chrysler
1968	David Pearson	Ford	1955	Tim Flock	Chrysler
1967	Richard Petty	Plymouth	1954	Lee Petty	Chrysler
1966	David Pearson	Dodge	1953	Herb Thomas	Hudson
1965	Ned Jarrett	Ford	1952	Tim Flock	Hudson
1964	Richard Petty	Plymouth	1951	Herb Thomas	Hudson
1963	Joe Weatherly	Pontiac	1950	Bill Rexford	Oldsmobile
1962	Joe Weatherly	Pontiac	1949	Red Byron	Oldsmobile

2016 NASCAR HALL OF FAME CLASS

Jerry Cook: Cook won six national championships in a division of NASCAR not seen often on national TV, the Modified races. These are more like open-wheel racing, but they operate on very small, tight tracks.

Bobby Isaac: He won 37 races at NASCAR's top level, with a high finish of second overall in 1968. Isaac excelled at capturing pole positions; he earned a record 19 in 1969.

Terry Labonte: If a NASCAR race started in the 1980s and 1990s, Labonte was in it. He started a then-record 665 straight races. He also won the NASCAR title in 1984 and 1996.

O. Bruton Smith: He made his mark by organizing races and running speedways. His company, Speedway Motorsports, owns eight NASCAR tracks. He also built the famous Charlotte Motor Speedway.

Curtis Turner: An early pioneer of stock car racing, Turner made his mark on dirt tracks and was part of NASCAR's first seasons starting in 1949.

OTHER MOTOR SPORTS

HIGH-SPEED BIKE!

MotoGP is one of the fastest sports on two wheels. Racers have to keep their balance while leaning into tight turns on twisting tracks. Spain's Marc Márquez is a two-time world champion in this exciting sport, which is much more popular around the world than in the U.S. However, one of MotoGP's annual races is this one, held in Austin, Texas.

Formula 1

Lewis Hamilton was out in front near the start at Abu Dhabi, and he was in front at the end, too!

Sebastian who? The disappearance of four-time champion **Sebastian Vettel** from the high ranks of Formula 1 created an exciting season-long race for the top spot. The 2014 drivers' championship came down to the final race in November in Abu Dhabi. By taking the checkered flag there, Britain's **Lewis Hamilton** won his second career F1 championship.

Nico Rosberg of Germany came into the race in second place and with a slight chance at the title, but engine trouble doomed those hopes. In fact, Hamilton pretty much put the race away with a lightning-quick start. Rosberg had earned the pole position in qualifying. That front-row spot vanished in seconds as Hamilton poured on the juice with a perfect start.

"It was like a rocket, probably the best start I've ever had," Hamilton said. "I knew straight away I was in the lead." He never gave it up. The 50 points for winning in Abu Dhabi gave him 384 for the season, 67 points ahead of Rosberg.

Abu Dhabi was Hamilton's 11th race victory of the season. He started the season almost as fast as he started the race Abu Dhabi, winning four of the first five races. Rosberg won two of the first six, and the race was on. Rosberg won in Monaco and Austria and was one victory shy of Hamilton to that point. Newcomer **Daniel Ricciardo** of Australia slipped in with wins at Canada, Hungary, and Belgium.

It looked like it would be a three-man race before the Italian Grand Prix in September. Rosberg led the way early, but Hamilton stayed close. Engine trouble and a bad turn cost Rosberg time and the British driver caught up. Hamilton's victory in Italy started a season-clinching five-race winning streak that was capped off with the checkered flag in the U.S. Grand Prix in Austin, Texas.

The U.S. win was a historic one for the driver from Stevenage, England. Formula 1 has a long history of great British drivers, including former world champions **Jackie Stewart**, **Stirling Moss**, and **Jim Clark**. Hamilton's Austin win gave him 32 for his career, the most by a driver from the United Kingdom. His season championship also tied Hamilton with Clark and **Graham Hill** for second most by a British driver behind Stewart's three.

So what happened to Vettel? He had been nearly unbeatable since winning his first title in 2010. Even in 2013, he had won an amazing 13 races. In 2014? Zero. However, racing experts pointed to new rules that began in 2014. To improve both driver safety and car performance, F1 changed the size of the engines and the amount of fuel each team could use in a race. Part of the reason for this was

Hamilton wore the Union Jack for the second time.

❝This is the greatest day of my life and it's really due to all the people around me.❞

— **LEWIS HAMILTON** THANKING HIS FORMULA 1 TEAM AFTER WINNING THE SEASON CHAMPIONSHIP IN ABU DHABI

the introduction of a high-tech system that charges a battery by harnessing the power of the brakes. The battery, together with the fuel, powers the engine. In other words, F1 cars became hybrids, like some of the cars you might see on the freeway. Finally, new car design rules took away some of the cars' downforce, or the air pressure that helps drivers maneuver through tight turns. Other drivers adjusted. Vettel didn't . . . and Hamilton roared to a season of success.

2014 F1 FINAL STANDINGS

PLACE/DRIVER	COUNTRY	TEAM	POINTS
1. **Lewis HAMILTON**	Great Britain	Mercedes AMG Petronas	384
2. **Nico ROSBERG**	Germany	Mercedes AMG Petronas	317
3. **Daniel RICCIARDO**	Australia	Infiniti Red Bull Racing	238
4. **Valtteri BOTTAS**	Finland	Williams Martini Racing	186
5. **Sebastian VETTEL**	Germany	Infiniti Red Bull Racing	167

2014 IndyCar

No one remembers who finished second in a race or in a season championship. That's why **Will Power** was so excited to earn his first IndyCar season title in 2014. The veteran driver from Australia had finished second from 2010–12. So close and yet so far!

He nearly lost it again in the final race of the season at Fontana, Calif. **Helio Castroneves** was chasing Power in the points race and was far ahead of Power in the day's race. But the Brazilian was penalized for going too fast in pit road. The penalty put him way back in the pack with no hope of catching Power.

"I don't believe it," Power said after the race. "I'm so mentally exhausted. My hands are numb from hanging on to the wheel so tight. I want to be so much more excited, but I'm just drained."

2014 VERIZON INDYCAR SERIES
FINAL STANDINGS

PLACE/DRIVER	POINTS
1. **Will POWER**	671
2. **Helio CASTRONEVES**	609
3. **Scott DIXON**	604
4. **Juan Pablo MONTOYA**	586
5. **Simon PAGENAUD**	565

Power had taken a solid points lead after winning the Milwaukee Mile two weeks earlier, setting up the final-race sprint for the title. That was his third race win of the season, including winning the season opener back in March in Florida. He was in the points hunt when he made a furious dash from the back of the pack to earn second-place points in Texas, a key turning point in his season.

In Toronto, veteran driver **Sébastien Bourdais** won his first race in seven seasons. When Power won the Milwaukee Mile on a large oval, he silenced some critics who had said he was just a road-course specialist. Winning on the oval put

Will Power had enough power in the season's final race to capture the title.

2015 INDY 500
Last Lap Drama

Fans at the 2015 Indy 500 got their money's worth. Three of the sport's top drivers battled neck and neck over the final few laps. In the end, **Juan Pablo Montoya** held off a fast-charging **Scott Dixon** and **Will Power** to win his second title at the race track known as "the Brickyard." Dixon and Power exchanged the lead several times late in the race. With three laps left, Montoya made a daring pass for the lead on Turn 4 as more than 300,000 fans screamed with excitement. All that was left was to get a nice sip of milk, an Indy 500 tradition.

Montoya made the most of his milk!

him in prime position to race for the title at Fontana. Power finished ninth, but he was far enough ahead of Castroneves that the title was his.

Tony Kanaan won that final California race. He was the eleventh different driver to win in the season, showing the growing depth of the IndyCar talent.

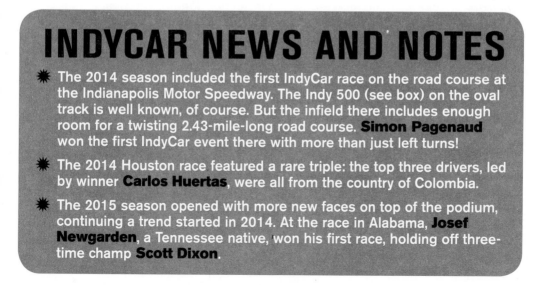

INDYCAR NEWS AND NOTES

* The 2014 season included the first IndyCar race on the road course at the Indianapolis Motor Speedway. The Indy 500 (see box) on the oval track is well known, of course. But the infield there includes enough room for a twisting 2.43-mile-long road course. **Simon Pagenaud** won the first IndyCar event there with more than just left turns!

* The 2014 Houston race featured a rare triple: the top three drivers, led by winner **Carlos Huertas**, were all from the country of Colombia.

* The 2015 season opened with more new faces on top of the podium, continuing a trend started in 2014. At the race in Alabama, **Josef Newgarden**, a Tennessee native, won his first race, holding off three-time champ **Scott Dixon**.

Drag Racing

Erica Enders-Stevens proved a power pioneer in winning Pro Stock.

TOP FUEL

The rock stars of drag racing are the skinny but super-powerful Top Fuel cars. With back tires that look like they come from a cartoon, the cars power down the straight at more than 300 miles per hour . . . in only 1,000 feet! In 2014, **Tony Schumacher** claimed his eighth NHRA Top Fuel season championship, the most by any driver. Schumacher had not won it all since 2009, so this was a return to the top for the champ.

PRO STOCK

While NASCAR's **Danica Patrick** gets most of the attention for female racers, drag racing is where the winning women really are. In 2014, women won 14 NHRA races. In Pro Stock, **Erica Enders-Stevens** became the first woman to claim the world championship. Enders-Stevens won six races on the season. She joins former Top Fuel champ **Shirley Muldowney** and Pro Stock Motorcycle winner **Angelle Sampey** as female season champs.

FUNNY CAR

For once, the Force was not with John. That is, the 16-time champion **John Force** did not add to his amazing career record. Instead, 2011 champ **Matt Hagan** outfoxed the old master. After winning three races in the season, Hagan clinched the title with a final-race victory at the Auto Club NHRA Finals in November. Who did he beat in that last race? None other than Force himself. "The championship was really what we were after, and the race win was kind of icing on the cake," Hagan said.

PRO STOCK MOTORCYCLE

Andrew Hines won three titles in this high-speed racing class, but his last one was way back in 2006. With an early-round victory on the final weekend of 2014, he got enough points to make his way back to the top of the world championship ranks. "I've been waiting a long time to put 'four-time' next to my name," he said after the race.

Motorcycle Racing

SUPERCROSS

Ryan Dungey dominated the field in 2015 to claim his second Supercross title. He finished in the top three of each of the final 13 races for the season, the longest such streak by a rider since 2007. He finished well ahead of **Eli Tomac** in the points chase. Dungey was behind early in the season to German star **Ken Roczen**, but an ankle injury kept Roczen off the bike after March. After Roczen went down, Dungey went off. He won six of the season's remaining eight races, including the final at Las Vegas. He finished second in the two he didn't win! Add in **Ryan Villopoto**'s wins since 2010 and there have been six straight Ryans atop the Supercross standings.

MOTOCROSS

Indoors or outdoors didn't matter to **Ryan Dungey**. After winning Supercross (mostly indoor races), he powered to the title in Motorcross (mostly outdoor races). In fact, he clinched the title with one race to go. At the Utah race, he won both motos to earn enough points to finish the season on top. Dungey had a strong finish to the season, winning the last five races on the schedule. **Ken Roczen** rebounded from injury to finish second overall. In the smaller-engine 250cc division, **Jeremy Martin** won his second straight championship, squeaking ahead of **Marvin Musquin**.

MOTOGP

While American riders specialize in dirt bikes on bumpy tracks, international riders hit high speeds on road tracks. The most famous series is called MotoGP (Grand Prix) like the famous auto races. Their season includes as many as 18 races at tracks in 13 countries, from Qatar to Germany and from Italy to Malaysia. Spain's **Marc Márquez** repeated as the season champion in 2014 with a remarkable 13 wins for the year.

Dungey powered to his second Supercross title.

Major Champions
OF THE 2000s

TOP FUEL DRAGSTERS

YEAR	DRIVER
2014	Tony Schumacher
2013	Shawn Langdon
2012	Antron Brown
2011	Del Worsham
2010	Larry Dixon
2009	Tony Schumacher
2008	Tony Schumacher
2007	Tony Schumacher
2006	Tony Schumacher
2005	Tony Schumacher
2004	Tony Schumacher
2003	Larry Dixon
2002	Larry Dixon
2001	Kenny Bernstein

FUNNY CARS

YEAR	DRIVER
2014	Matt Hagan
2013	John Force
2012	Jack Beckman
2011	Matt Hagan
2010	John Force
2009	Robert Hight
2008	Cruz Pedregon
2007	Tony Pedregon
2006	John Force
2005	Gary Scelzi
2004	John Force
2003	Tony Pedregon
2002	John Force
2001	John Force

PRO STOCK CARS

YEAR	DRIVER
2014	Erica Enders-Stevens
2013	Jeg Coughlin Jr.
2012	Allen Johnson
2011	Jason Line
2010	Greg Anderson
2009	Mike Edwards
2008	Jeg Coughlin Jr.
2007	Jeg Coughlin Jr.
2006	Jason Line
2005	Greg Anderson
2004	Greg Anderson
2003	Greg Anderson
2002	Jeg Coughlin Jr.
2001	Warren Johnson

FORMULA ONE

YEAR	DRIVER
2014	Lewis Hamilton
2013	Sebastian Vettel
2012	Sebastian Vettel
2011	Sebastian Vettel
2010	Sebastian Vettel
2009	Jenson Button
2008	Lewis Hamilton
2007	Kimi Räikkönen
2006	Fernando Alonso
2005	Fernando Alonso
2004	Michael Schumacher
2003	Michael Schumacher
2002	Michael Schumacher
2001	Michael Schumacher

INDYCAR SERIES

YEAR	DRIVER
2014	**Will Power**
2013	**Scott Dixon**
2012	**Ryan Hunter-Reay**
2011	**Dario Franchitti**
2010	**Dario Franchitti**
2009	**Dario Franchitti**
2008	**Scott Dixon**
2007	**Dario Franchitti**
2006	**Sam Hornish Jr.**
2005	**Dan Wheldon**
2004	**Tony Kanaan**
2003	**Scott Dixon**
2002	**Sam Hornish Jr.**
2001	**Sam Hornish Jr.**

AMA SUPERCROSS

YEAR	DRIVER
2015	**Ryan Dungey**
2014	**Ryan Villopoto**
2013	**Ryan Villopoto**
2012	**Ryan Villopoto**
2011	**Ryan Villopoto**
2010	**Ryan Dungey**
2009	**James Stewart Jr.**
2008	**Chad Reed**
2007	**James Stewart Jr.**
2006	**Ricky Carmichael**
2005	**Ricky Carmichael**
2004	**Chad Reed**
2003	**Ricky Carmichael**
2002	**Ricky Carmichael**
2001	**Ricky Carmichael**

AMA MOTOCROSS

YEAR	RIDER (MOTOCROSS)	RIDER (LITES)
2014	**Ryan Dungey**	**Jeremy Martin**
2014	**Ken Roczen**	**Jeremy Martin**
2013	**Ryan Villopoto**	**Eli Tomac**
2012	**Ryan Dungey**	**Blake Baggett**
2011	**Ryan Villopoto**	**Dean Wilson**
2010	**Ryan Dungey**	**Trey Canard**
2009	**Chad Reed**	**Ryan Dungey**
2008	**James Stewart Jr.**	**Ryan Villopoto**
2007	**Grant Langston**	**Ryan Villopoto**
2006	**Ricky Carmichael**	**Ryan Villopoto**
2005	**Ricky Carmichael**	**Ivan Tedesco**
2004	**Ricky Carmichael**	**James Stewart Jr.**
2003	**Ricky Carmichael**	**Grant Langston**
2002	**Ricky Carmichael**	**James Stewart Jr.**
2001	**Ricky Carmichael**	**Mike Brown**

ACTION SPORTS

UP, UP, AND AWAY!
Men's ski superpipe athlete Gus Kenworthy got some big air during his event at the Winter X Games. Hundreds of action stars poured into Aspen, Colorado, to try to take home medals. Kenworthy only finished fifth, but for more on the winners, read on!

Summer X Games

Broken arm and all, Burnquist won Big Air.

29 ... and Counting

When the X Games began in 1995, skateboarder **Bob Burnquist** was there. He was there when the X Games were held in Austin, Texas, in 2015—and he was there for every year in between. So he wasn't about to let a little thing like a cast on his broken arm keep him from winning career medals No. 28 (gold in Skateboard Big Air) and No. 29 (gold, with **Morgan Wade**, in the first Skate/BMX Big Air Doubles event). In fact, the 38-year-old credited the injury, suffered during practice the day before the X Games began, for giving him a little extra fire to power through when things weren't perfect.

*"It's just an arm.
If it were a leg or something,
that'd be different."*

–VETERAN SKATEBOARD STAR **BOB BURNQUIST**, AFTER BREAKING HIS ARM SHORTLY BEFORE THE 2015 X GAMES IN AUSTIN. BURNQUIST WENT ON TO WIN GOLD IN THE BIG AIR AND BIG AIR DOUBLES COMPETITIONS.

Teen Driver

When the light turned green, **Sheldon Creed** put pedal to the metal and never looked back while winning the Off-Road Truck Racing competition at the 2015 X Games. Creed outlasted a finals field that included such experienced drivers as 46-year-old **Robby Gordon**, 33-year-old **Arie Luyendyk Jr.**, and 31-year-old X Games legend **Travis Pastrana**. Also in the competition, but not advancing to the

2015 SUMMER X GAMES CHAMPS

BMX

BIG AIR	COLTON SATTERFIELD
DIRT	KYLE BALDOCK
PARK	DANIEL SANDOVAL
VERT	VINCE BYRON

MOTO X

BEST WHIP	JARRYD MCNEIL
ENDURO (MEN)	MIKE BROWN
ENDURO (WOMEN)	LAIA SANZ
FLAT TRACK	BRYAN SMITH
QUARTERPIPE	TOM PAGES
SPEED & STYLE	NATE ADAMS
STEP UP	RONNIE RENNER

RALLYING

OFF-ROAD TRUCK RACING	SHELDON CREED
RALLYCROSS	SCOTT SPEED

SKATEBOARDING

BIG AIR	BOB BURNQUIST
VERT	PIERRE-LUC GAGNON
VERT BEST TRICK	ELLIOT SLOAN
PARK	CURREN CAPLES
STREET AMATEURS	TYSON BOWERBANK
STREET (MEN)	NYJAH HUSTON
STREET (WOMEN)	ALEXIS SABLONE

SKATE/BMX

BIG AIR DOUBLES	MORGAN WADE/ BOB BURNQUIST

finals, was 58-year-old **Rusty Wallace**, a NASCAR Hall of Famer. Did we mention Creed was just 17 years old? In case you're wondering, Creed got his actual driver's license in October 2013, shortly after he turned 16 years old.

Huston Takes Austin

Skateboarder **Nyjah Huston** had dominated Street for months leading up to the X Games, but then he lost a key even in the spring in Tampa. That was back in March 2015. Huston didn't lose again, though, and was back in his familiar spot atop the podium in Austin in June. His 11-point victory in Street marked his seventh X Games gold medal.

X Games Notes

* Skateboarder **Alexis Sablone** has a bachelor's degree from Columbia University and a graduate degree from MIT. She also won her second gold medal in Street Skating.

* The longest winning streak in X Games history ended when **Vince Byron** toppled nine-time winner Jamie Bestwick in BMX Vert.

* Where's the Snow? The quarter-pipe is a familiar sight at the Winter X Games, but a dirt pipe debuted at the first Moto X QuarterPipe competition in Austin. **Tom Pagès** won it.

Winter X Games

With a bandage on her face and a snowboard on her feet, 14-year-old Chloe Kim was a winner.

The Future Is Now

"In years to come, I'll be able to look at women's snowboarding and know that not only is it in good hands, but it's in the hands of someone I'm proud of," **Kelly Clark** said before the Winter X Games in Aspen, Colorado, in 2015. Clark, who was going after her sixth consecutive gold medal in the Snowboard SuperPipe, was talking about **Chloe Kim**, among others. In 2014, the then-13-year-old Kim was second to Clark in the SuperPipe at the X Games. In 2015, Kim was second to Clark again . . . until she took off on her final run. Then she nailed her run to overcome Clark and win the gold. At 14, Kim was the youngest winner ever at the X Games.

Eight-Peat

There's no such thing as a sure thing in sports, of course, but snowmobiling's **Tucker Hibbert** is about as close as it gets. The most dominant rider in SnoCross history, Hibbert breezed to a 20-second victory in the 20-lap race at the X Games in 2015. It was his eighth consecutive X Games win and his ninth gold medal in all. His 13 career medals in SnoCross equal the most of any Winter X Games competitor in a given discipline. One week later, in Deadwood, South Dakota, Hibbert notched another milestone when he raced to his 100th career Pro National SnoCross victory.

Oh, Canada!

It's all pretty cool stuff at the X Games, but nothing got the crowd going in Aspen quite like the men's Ski SuperPipe competition. "I realized throughout the contest that they were rewarding big for [height] and I was like, 'All right, I got to step up my game a little bit,'" said Aspen native **Alex Ferreira**. He stepped up all right, soaring more than 20 feet above the half-pipe and earning a bronze medal. **Kevin Rolland** went even higher (23 feet) to take the silver. **Simon d'Artois** didn't get quite that much air (21 feet 6 inches), but he executed a perfect double-cork 1080 to wow the judges and become the first Canadian to win the event.

"My face kind of hurts right now."

–FOURTEEN-YEAR-OLD **CHLOE KIM**, WHEN ASKED HOW SHE FELT AFTER WINNING THE SNOWBOARD SUPERPIPE. KIM HAD SMASHED HER FACE AGAINST THE SNOW WHILE WIPING OUT ON HER FINAL PRACTICE RUN.

Eye in the Sky

Not all of the innovation at the X Games came on the snow-covered slopes and tracks. Some of it came above the ground, where custom-built drones delivered all-new views of the action. Television audiences got to see snowboarders and snowmobilers from amazing new vantage points and angles. The 25-pound drones, which measured about 40 inches in diameter, could fly behind, over, or in front of the competitors as they raced over bumps at high speed and launched into gravity-defying jumps.

2015 WINTER X GAMES CHAMPS

Event	Champion	Event	Champion
MONO SKIER X	Chris DEVLIN-YOUNG	W SNOWBOARD SUPERPIPE	Chloe KIM
SKI BIG AIR	Vincent GAGNIER	M SNOWBOARDER X	Kevin HILL
M SKI SLOPESTYLE	Nick GOEPPER	W SNOWBOARDER X	Lindsey JACOBELLIS
W SKI SLOPESTYLE	Emma DAHLSTRÖM	SNOWBOARDER X ADAPTIVE	Keith GABEL
M SKI SUPERPIPE	Simon D'ARTOIS	SNOWMOBILE HILLCROSS	Ryan SIMONS
W SKI SUPERPIPE	Maddie BOWMAN	SNOWMOBILE LONG JUMP	Heath FRISBY
M SNOWBOARD BIG AIR	Mark MCMORRIS	SNOWMOBILE SNOCROSS	Tucker HIBBERT
M SNOWBOARD SLOPESTYLE	Mark MCMORRIS	SNOWMOBILE SNOCROSS ADAPTIVE	Garrett GOODWIN
W SNOWBOARD SLOPESTYLE	Silje NORENDAL	SNOWMOBILE SPEED & STYLE	Colten MOORE
M SNOWBOARD SUPERPIPE	Danny DAVIS		

Action Notes

Beach Boys

Gabriel Medina began surfing at age 9 in his native Brazil, and by 11 earned his first national championship. A decade later, he became a world champion when he won the Association of Surfing Professionals (ASP) Tour for the 2014 season. Medina outdistanced defending champ Mick Fanning of Australia for the title. The top American finisher was the legendary Kelly Slater, who was fourth. (At 42, Slater, who has won a record 11 ASP World titles in his amazing career, was twice as old as the champ.)

When Medina got off to a slow start in 2015, fellow countryman Adriano De Souza posted top-three finishes in each of the season's first three events to vault to the top of the standings.

Brazilian Gabriel Medina showed all the right moves in becoming the 2014 ASP champ.

Battle of the Aussies

In women's surfing, Australian **Stephanie Gilmore** won the ASP world title for the sixth time since 2007 in what the organization called "the most intense Championship battle in the history of professional surfing." Gilmore finished in fifth place in the final event on the WCT calendar in Hawaii. That gave her just enough points to edge fellow Aussie **Tyler Wright**, who was second to Honolulu's **Carissa Moore** in the event. Had Wright won the event, she and Gilmore would have finished in a tie for the overall lead, with the champ determined by a surf-off.

Moore followed her big finish in 2014 by getting off to a great start in 2015. She posted four top-threes in a row to take the overall points lead.

> *"I felt like a rock star!"*
>
> –HIGH DIVER **ORLANDO DUQUE**, ON THE RECEPTION HE RECEIVED FROM THE FANS WHEN THE 2015 RED BULL WORLD SERIES OPENED IN CARTAGENA IN HIS NATIVE COLOMBIA. DEFENDING SEASON CHAMP **GARY HUNT** WON THE EVENT. DUQUE FINISHED THIRD.

BOARD SPORT

Curren Caples, who was named after former world surfing champion Tom Curren, enjoys spending time on a board himself. But his best moves are on a skateboard. Caples turned pro at age 17 in 2013, and won the gold medal in Street at X Games Munich that year. Caples opened the 2015 Dew Tour season with a victory in Skateboard Streetstyle in Chicago. And, yes, Caples does like to surf, too.

Maddo's World

Motorcyclist **Robbie "Maddo" Maddison** has jumped onto a replica of the Arc de Triomphe in Las Vegas, leaped the width of the Corinth Canal in Greece, and soared over San Diego Bay in California. So why not launch his bike off a ski jump? You mean besides the fact that it was an 18½-story drop, with no snow to cushion the fall? Maddison never let little details like that stop him, though, so in November 2014 he took off from the ski jump in Olympic Park in Park City, Utah. Not only did Maddison drop 185 feet, but he also soared a length of 374 feet. That's just slightly longer than a football field from the back of one end zone to the back of the other. Maddison stuck the landing perfectly!

GOLF

ALL SMILES
You'd smile, too, if you were just 21 years old and already a two-time golf major winner, like American star Jordan Spieth.

America's Got Talent

A chance at golf history slid by when **Jordan Spieth's** birdie try on the final hole of the 2015 British Open settled just a few inches wide of the hole. Spieth needed to make that long putt from just off the green to join a playoff and keep alive his hopes to become the first golfer in 62 years to win the first three majors of the season: the Masters, the US Open, and the British Open. No men's golfer ever has won the modern Grand Slam (each of the year's four majors, including the PGA Championship).

After missing the putt, Spieth buried his face in his hands. Later, he admitted, "It stings a little bit." Still, there was nothing for Spieth to hang his head over after a fantastic 2015 season in which he established himself as the leader of a new generation of top American golfers—and threatened **Rory McIlroy's** status as the top player in the world.

After several top-10 showings early in the season, Spieth reeled off an amazing four-tournament stretch in the spring in which he posted two wins and two second-place finishes. He capped the string with his first major title at the Masters championship.

In a dominating performance at Augusta National, the Texan equaled the tournament scoring record first set by **Tiger Woods** in 1997. Spieth fired a 64 in the opening round to take the lead. He sailed to a wire-to-wire win, winning by four strokes. At 21 years old, he was the second-youngest Masters champ (behind only Woods, who also was 21 in 1997, but six months younger).

If anyone believed Spieth's Masters win was a fluke, he put those thoughts to rest with major victory No. 2 at the US Open in June. That one was a lot closer, though. Spieth was among four players tied for the lead entering the final round at Chambers Bay in Washington. He birdied the final hole to outlast **Dustin Johnson** and **Louis Oosthuizen** by one shot.

By the time the British Open at Scotland's historic St. Andrews rolled around in July, Spieth was ranked No. 2 in the world, behind only Northern Ireland's McIlroy. Fellow Americans **Bubba Watson**, **Dustin Johnson**, **Rickie Fowler**, and **Jim Furyk** rounded out the top six. But it was another American, **Zach Johnson**, who emerged from a large pack of players to hoist the championship trophy called the Claret Jug.

Spieth rounded out his truly remarkable year by finishing as the runner-up at the PGA Championship, behind first-time winner **Jason Day** from Australia.

2015 MEN'S MAJORS

THE MASTERS
Jordan Spieth

THE U.S. OPEN
Jordan Spieth

THE BRITISH OPEN
Zach Johnson

THE PGA CHAMPIONSHIP
Jason Day

The Ryder Cup

America may have a ton of individual talent, but Europe proved to still be the best at team golf when it successfully defended its title at the prestigious Ryder Cup competition in the fall of 2014.

The US has an all-time record of 25–13–2 in the Ryder Cup, but Europe easily won the 2014 event at Gleneagles in Scotland, 16.5 to 11.5. English star **Justin Rose** produced four points in his five matches, winning three times and tying twice.

The Ryder Cup is the top team golf event in the world. With a few exceptions, it has been held every two years since 1927, when it began as a competition between men's teams from the United States and Great Britain. The Great Britain side expanded to include all of continental Europe in 1979.

The Ryder Cup is a three-day, match-play event. Golfers compete in several different types of games, wrapping up with 12 one-on-one singles matches on the final Sunday. Each match counts as one point for the winning team. A tie means half a point for each side.

The next Ryder Cup will be held in 2016 at the Hazeltine National Golf Club in Chaska, Minnesota. The US team is hoping home-course advantage can help them get the Cup back.

2014 US RYDER CUP TEAM

CAPTAIN: **Tom Watson**

Keegan Bradley	Phil Mickelson
Rickie Fowler	Patrick Reed
Jim Furyk	Webb Simpson
Zach Johnson	Jordan Spieth
Matt Kuchar	Jimmy Walker
Hunter Mahan	Bubba Watson

Rose was bloomin' happy to win.

Chip Shots

Sand Save ▶

Robert Streb casually tossed his putter toward his golf bag midway through the final round of the Greenbrier Classic in 2015–only to see the putter snap between the shaft and the clubhead. "Huh, that's not good," Streb thought.

Turns out it was not so bad, either. Forced to use a sand wedge on the greens for a makeshift putter, Streb buried five birdies on the back nine, including one on the 18th hole, to qualify for a four-man, sudden-death playoff.

PGA rules allowed Streb to go back to his locker before the playoff to replace his broken putter. Ironically, a couple of bad shots on the first playoff hole meant he was eliminated before he could even use the new putter.

Class of 2011

That was the year **Jordan Spieth** graduated . . . from high school. The amazing thing is, the young Texan wasn't the only 2011 high school graduate to make a big splash on the PGA Tour in 2015.

Remember these names, too: **Daniel Berger**, **Justin Thomas**, and **Ollie Schniederjans**. By midway through his rookie season in 2015, Florida's Berger already had posted several top-10 finishes, including the Honda Classic, where he finished second in a playoff to three-time major winner **Padraig Harrington**. Thomas, from Kentucky, nearly won the John Deere Classic in July before one bad hole on Sunday dropped him to fifth place. Texas-born and Georgia-bred Schniederjans, the top-ranked amateur in the world in 2014, turned pro after finishing in a tie for 12th at the British Open in 2015.

Bad Break

It takes a good break here and there to win any golf tournament, let alone a major championship. But world No. 1 **Rory McIlroy** got a bad break in 2015 that kept him from defending his British Open championship. Well, not a break, but a torn ligament in his ankle that sidelined McIlroy from the tournament he won in 2014.

With two wins and four other top-10 finishes in eight starts, McIlroy was having another terrific season in the lead-up to the 2015 British Open at St. Andrews. His injury came just two weeks before the tournament. The Irishman was playing soccer with some friends when he got hurt.

More Chip Shots

Bonus Baby

The FedEx Cup is the PGA Tour's season-long points race. The chase ends with the FedEx Cup playoffs, a string of four tournaments that begins with 125 players. The field is narrowed each week. The winner of the 30-man, season-ending Tour Championship takes home a cool $10 million bonus.

Billy Horschel was ranked No. 69 as the 2014 FedEx Cup playoffs began and missed the cut at The Barclays Championship. But then he played his next 12 rounds with scores in the 60s. Talk about getting hot at the right time! Horschel tied for second at the Deutsche Bank Championship, then captured the BMW Championship. That gave him a spot in the following weeks's Tour Championship, which he won by three shots to earn the $10 million bonus.

Two days after winning the FedEx Cup, Horschel became the father of a new baby

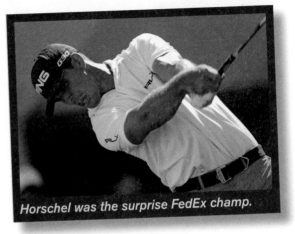
Horschel was the surprise FedEx champ.

girl. She is going to have some really, really nice baby clothes!

Rory McIlroy won't have any trouble paying for new duds, either. Rory won the PGA money title for 2014 (the money title doesn't include bonuses) with just under $8.3 million. A huge chunk of that came while winning three straight tournaments that summer that included two majors, the British Open and the PGA Championship.

OTHER WINNERS

The PGA Tour has other groups of players competing for a title.

Champions Tour German native **Bernhard Langer** is a golfing machine who keeps on humming year after year. He won the Charles Schwab Cup—the equivalent of the FedEx Cup for the Champions Tour and the over-50 crowd—in 2014 by a wide margin over British star **Colin Montgomerie**. Langer posted 18 top-10 finishes, including five wins. At 56, the two-time Masters champ also tied for eighth at that tournament in April of 2014.

Web.com Tour Younger players often work their way up to the PGA Tour after getting their start on the Web.com Tour. Think of it as the highest level of golf's minor leagues, where you'll see tomorrow's stars today. Web.com players fight to finish in the top 25 of the season-long standings to earn a spot on the PGA Tour for the following year. **Adam Hadwin** topped that group in the 2014 season.

LPGA Update

TEEN STAR! ▶▶▶

Quick, name the youngest player ever to be ranked No. 1 in the world in professional golf. **Tiger Woods**? **Rory McIlroy**? **Jordan Spieth**? All good guesses, but the answer is 17-year-old **Lydia Ko**. A native of South Korea and a resident of New Zealand, Ko reached that lofty perch early in the 2015 season.

Ko was the top-ranked amateur in the world for more than two and a half years and won a pair of LPGA Tour events before turning pro in October of 2013, just six months after her 16th birthday. She won three times on tour in 2014 to earn LPGA Rookie of the Year honors. Shortly after reaching No. 1 in 2015, she won the Australian Open, too.

Ko is "exceptionally talented, mature beyond her years, and well liked by golf fans and competitors alike," says former world No. 1 **Annika Sörenstam**.

LIGHTNING STRIKES

Lightning struck twice just moments apart for South Korean–born **Sei Young Kim** at the Lotte Championship in Hawaii in the spring of 2015. First, she chipped in on the 18th hole of the final round to force a sudden-death playoff with **Inbee Park**. Then, on the same hole in the playoff, Kim faced a 154-yard shot. It just cleared the water, took two hops, and disappeared into the cup for an unlikely victory.

As incredible as that shot was, it wasn't the most dramatic of Kim's career. She once won a tournament in Korea by making a hole-in-one on No. 17 in the final round.

FIRST TIME IS A CHARM

U.S. Open golf tournaments—whether men's or women's—are brutal tests of golf in which a par is a good score. Players aren't supposed to make four birdies on the back nine on Sunday. But that's exactly what **In Gee Chun** did in the final round to win the season's second major in the summer of 2015. Chun carded birdies on 12, 15, 16, and 17 to outlast second-place **Amy Yang** by one shot.

LPGA MAJOR WINNERS

ANA Inspiration	**Brittany Lincicome**
U.S. Women's Open	**In Gee Chun**
KPMG Women's PGA Championship	**Inbee Park**
RICOH Women's British Open	**Inbee Park**
The Evian Championship	**Lydia Ko**

The Majors

In golf, some tournaments are known as the Majors. They're the most important events of the year on the men's and women's pro tours. (There are four men's Majors and five women's Majors.) Among the men, Jack Nicklaus holds the record for the most all-time wins in the Majors. Patty Berg won more Majors than any other women's player.

MEN'S

	MASTERS	US OPEN	BRITISH OPEN	PGA CHAMP.	TOTAL
Jack **NICKLAUS**	6	4	3	5	**18**
Tiger **WOODS**	4	3	3	4	**14**
Walter **HAGEN**	0	2	4	5	**11**
Ben **HOGAN**	2	4	1	2	**9**
Gary **PLAYER**	3	1	3	2	**9**
Tom **WATSON**	2	1	5	0	**8**
Arnold **PALMER**	4	1	2	0	**7**
Gene **SARAZEN**	1	2	1	3	**7**
Sam **SNEAD**	3	0	1	3	**7**
Harry **VARDON**	0	1	6	0	**7**

PAST 10 WINNERS OF THE RYDER CUP

YEAR	WINNING TEAM (SCORE)	YEAR	WINNING TEAM (SCORE)
2014	EUROPE (16.5-11.5)	2004	EUROPE (18.5-9.5)
2012	EUROPE (14.5-13.5)	2002	EUROPE (15.5-12.5)
2010	EUROPE (14.5-13.5)	1999	UNITED STATES (14.5-13.5)
2008	UNITED STATES (16.5-11.5)	1997	EUROPE (14.5-13.5)
2006	EUROPE (18.5-9.5)	1995	EUROPE (14.5-13.5)

WOMEN'S

	LPGA	USO	BO	NAB	MAUR	TH	WES	TOTAL
Patty **BERG**	0	1	x	x	x	7	7	**15**
Mickey **WRIGHT**	4	4	x	x	x	2	3	**13**
Louise **SUGGS**	1	2	x	x	x	4	4	**11**
Annika **SÖRENSTAM**	3	3	1	3	x	x	x	**10**
Babe **ZAHARIAS**	x	3	x	x	x	3	4	**10**
Betsy **RAWLS**	2	4	x	x	x	x	2	**8**
Juli **INKSTER**	2	2	x	2	1	x	x	**7**
Karrie **WEBB**	1	2	1	2	1	x	x	**7**

KEY: LPGA = LPGA Championship, USO = US Open, BO = British Open, NAB = Nabisco Championship, MAUR = du Maurier (1979–2000), TH = Titleholders (1937–1972), WES = Western Open (1937–1967)

PGA TOUR CAREER EARNINGS*

1. Tiger Woods — $109,837,612
2. Phil Mickelson — $77,200,795
3. Vijay Singh — $69,226,213
4. Jim Furyk — $64,330,815
5. Ernie Els — $48,094,479
6. Davis Love III — $43,065,999
7. David Toms — $40,931,764
8. Steve Stricker — $40,876,420
9. Sergio Garcia — $40,321,748
10. Adam Scott — $38,613,516

LPGA TOUR CAREER EARNINGS*

1. Annika Sörenstam — $22,573,192
2. Karrie Webb — $19,586,588
3. Cristie Kerr — $16,634,899
4. Lorena Ochoa — $14,863,331
5. Juli Inkster — $13,807,099

*Through July 2015

TIGER WOODS

It was a rough year in the majors for former world No. 1 Tiger Woods in 2015. After a respectable tie for 17th place at the Masters, the former world No. 1 missed the cut at the U.S. Open and the British Open and fell to No. 258 in the world. Still, with 14 career victories in the majors, Woods ranks second only to **Jack Nicklaus** (18) on the all-time list. He and Nicklaus also are the only two players to win each of the four majors at least three times.

TENNIS

SUPERSTAR
Serena Williams continued to power her way upward on the list of all-time tennis greats. Her first three Grand Slam wins of 2015 moved her to third place all-time.

Serena Slam!

The four major tournaments on the pro tennis schedule—the Australia Open, French Open, Wimbledon, and the US Open—are known as the Grand Slam titles. Winning all four in one year is one of the most difficult accomplishments in sports, and is collectively known as the Grand Slam. Holding all four titles at the same time, but over two different seasons . . . well, no one really has a name for that. So when American star **Serena Williams** added the 2015 Australian, French, and Wimbledon titles to her 2014 US Open championship, it was dubbed the Serena Slam.

It seemed hard to believe by year's end, but at the start of 2015, four players—Serena Williams, **Maria Sharapova**, **Simona Halep**, and **Petra Kvitová**—all could make a case for being the top women's player in the world. But Williams put any doubts to rest with a 6–3, 7–6 (7–5) victory over Sharapova to win the Australian Open for the sixth time. It was her 19th Grand Slam title in all.

Win No. 20 came at the French Open in June, though not without a challenge from 13th-seeded **Lucie Safarova** of the

Serena needs a really, really big trophy case!

Czech Republic. Safarova entered the final on an upset roll, including a win over defending-champ Sharapova in Round 4. But Williams ended the run with a 6–3, 6–7 (7–2), 6–2 win.

In July, the 33-year-old Williams beat Spain's 21-year-old **Garbiñe Muguruza** in straight sets in the final at Wimbledon to complete the Serena Slam. Along the way, Williams beat her sister Venus in the fourth round, and ended Sharapova's hopes for her first Wimbledon title since 2004 in the semifinal. It was the sixth time Williams won at Wimbledon.

In September, she went for the Grand Slam but fell short. In one of the biggest sports upsets ever, Serena lost to unseeded Italian player **Roberta Vinci** in the semifinals. Though a stunning loss, it didn't take away from a magical year by Serena.

2015 WOMEN'S GRAND SLAMS

AUSTRALIAN OPEN	**Serena Williams**
FRENCH OPEN	**Serena Williams**
WIMBLEDON	**Serena Williams**
US OPEN	**Flavia Pannetta**

Men's Tennis

Djokovic has his eye on being the world's best.

In the future, experts might look back at this era as a Golden Age in men's tennis. Instead of just one or two young superstars dominating the game, fans are being treated to a host of players who can step up to win any major tournament. Today's stars include Serbia's **Novak Djokovic**, Switzerland's **Roger Federer** and **Stan Wawrinka**, Spain's **Rafael Nadal**, **Andy Murray** of the United Kingdom, and more.

If anyone was at the head of that class in 2015, it was Djokovic. In July, the top-ranked player in the world breezed past No. 2 Federer in four sets to win his second consecutive Wimbledon championship, and his third Grand Slam event in the last five.

Djokovic got the Grand Slam portion of the year off to a good start when he won the Australian Open for the fifth time. As the top seed in the tournament, he cruised through the first five rounds, winning every set, to earn the right to face defending-champ Wawrinka in the semifinals. Djokovic ousted Wawrinka in a five-set marathon. Then, just as he did in both 2011 and 2013, Djokovic easily beat Murray in the final. He won in four sets, including 6–0 in the final set.

Wawrinka got his revenge at the French Open several months later, beating Djokovic in four sets to win at Roland Garros for the first time. That was even after Djokovic stunned Nadal, nine-time winner of the French Open and current favorite in the quarterfinals.

In July, Federer was trying to become the first man to win the singles title at Wimbledon eight times. But after beating Murray (the 2013 champ) in the semifinals, the 34-year-old was no match for the 28-year-old Djokovic in the final. Djokovic became the first player to successfully defend his Wimbledon championship since Federer won his fifth Wimbledon title in a row in 2007.

At the US Open in September, the amazing Djokovic made it three out of four Grand Slams. He beat Federer in a matchup of the top two seeds. The win gave Djokovic his tenth career Grand Slam title.

2015 MEN'S GRAND SLAMS

AUSTRALIAN OPEN	**Novak Djokovic**
FRENCH OPEN	**Stan Wawrinka**
WIMBLEDON	**Novak Djokovic**
US OPEN	**Novak Djokovic**

Tennis Notes

Double Play

Martina Hingis was just 16 years old when she won the singles championship at Wimbledon in 1997. She was just 17 when she won the women's doubles crown for the second time in 1998. But that seemed like a lifetime ago when the Swiss star, now 34, teamed with India's **Sania Mirza** to win the doubles title again at Wimbledon in 2015.

Hingis, who was ranked No. 1 in the world for 209 weeks, had been forced to retire from singles play because of injuries, but has discovered a new career in doubles.

Trivia Time

Question: What are the five pro sports leagues in the United States to play 40 or more seasons?

Answer: Major League Baseball, the NFL, the NBA, the NHL . . . and World TeamTennis. That's right, World TeamTennis joined an elite group when it played season No. 40 in the summer of 2015.

In the early days of World TeamTennis–the league began in 1974, but did not play in 1979 or 1980–players included superstars **Billie Jean King**, **Chris Evert**, **Jimmy Connors**, **John McEnroe**, and more.

In 2015, young stars such as **Eugenie Bouchard** and **Madison Keys** joined veterans like **John Isner**, **Andy Roddick**, and **Venus** and **Serena Williams** in World TeamTennis.

The Washington Kastles won the league championship for the fifth straight time in 2015, defeating the Austin Aces in the final.

ONE FOR THE SWISS

The Davis Cup is the top international men's team tennis event in the world. (The women have a similar event called the Fed Cup.) The Davis Cup began in 1900 as a competition between the United States and Great Britain and has grown to include about 130 nations today. The top 16 countries compete in a single-elimination tournament for the title.

The United States has won the most Davis Cup championships (32). In 2014, Switzerland won their first when **Roger Federer** defeated France's **Richard Gasquet** in the clinching singles match. Nice to have the world's No. 2-ranked player on your team!

Grand Slams

ALL-TIME GRAND SLAM CHAMPIONSHIPS (MEN)

	AUS. OPEN	FRENCH OPEN	WIMBLEDON	US OPEN	TOTAL
Roger **FEDERER**	4	1	7	5	17
Rafael **NADAL**	1	9	2	2	14
Pete **SAMPRAS**	2	0	7	5	14
Roy **EMERSON**	6	2	2	2	12
Bjorn **BORG**	0	6	5	0	11
Rod **LAVER**	3	2	4	2	11
Bill **TILDEN**	0	0	3	7	10
Novak **DJOKOVIC**	5	0	3	2	10
Andre **AGASSI**	4	1	1	2	8
Jimmy **CONNORS**	1	0	2	5	8
Ivan **LENDL**	2	3	0	3	8
Fred **PERRY**	1	1	3	3	8
Ken **ROSEWALL**	4	2	0	2	8

JIMMY CONNORS

One of US tennis's all-time greats, Jimmy Connors was the top-ranked men's player in the world for much of the 1970s. Connors was a gritty, brash player whose antics stirred up the crowd and sometimes rubbed opponents (not to mention tennis officials!) the wrong way. But there was no denying his prowess on the court. He won 109 career championships, including eight Grand Slam titles, and set a record (since broken) when he held the top spot in the world rankings for 160 consecutive weeks from 1974 to 1977. He was at his best in the US Open, which he won five times.

ALL-TIME GRAND SLAM CHAMPIONSHIPS (WOMEN)

	AUS.	FRENCH	WIMBLEDON	US	TOTAL
Margaret Smith **COURT**	11	5	3	5	24
Steffi **GRAF**	4	6	7	5	22
Serena **WILLIAMS**	6	3	6	6	21
Helen Wills **MOODY**	0	4	8	7	19
Chris **EVERT**	2	7	3	6	18
Martina **NAVRATILOVA**	3	2	9	4	18
Billie Jean **KING**	1	1	6	4	12
Maureen **CONNOLLY**	1	2	3	3	9
Monica **SELES**	4	3	0	2	9
Suzanne **LENGLEN**	0	2*	6	0	8
Molla Bjurstedt **MALLORY**	0	0	0	8	8

*Also won four French titles before 1925; in those years, the tournament was open only to French nationals.

Maureen Connolly

In 1953, American Maureen Connolly became the first women's tennis player to complete the Grand Slam, winning all four major tournaments in the same calendar year. "Little Mo," who stood just 5 feet 5 inches, was only 18 years old when she won the Grand Slam. She won nine Grand Slam tournaments in four years from 1951 to 1954. But her career ended at 19 wins when a leg injury suffered while horseback riding forced her to retire.

Women's Grand Slam Champs
(single calendar year)

Maureen **CONNOLLY**	1953
Margaret **SMITH COURT**	1970
Steffi **GRAF**	1988

WINNER! WINNER! WINNER!
For the first time in 37 years, one of American sports' greatest prizes was captured. American Pharoah, with jockey Victor Espinoza, galloped to victory here in the Belmont Stakes. That gave the horse the coveted Triple Crown.

OTHER SPORTS

Cricket World Cup

When a billion people pay attention to something, it's worth checking out. Even more than that many people tuned in during the 2015 ICC World Cup to watch national teams play cricket. Not the insect, of course, the bat-and-ball game that is enormously popular in places such as England, Australia, India, Pakistan, and the West Indies. Cricket was born in Britain, and as Britain colonized lands around the world, it took its game along. Though the nations that play are now all independent, they kept their love and passion for the game.

Cricket might be described as baseball with only two bases. An important difference is that after a batter hits the ball, he doesn't have to run. But when he and his partner batsman do, they score runs for their team. Also, there are no balls and strikes. Instead, the pitcher, or bowler, is trying to knock over wooden sticks behind the batter. The batter is trying to protect them. There's a lot more to it than that, but those are the basics.

Fourteen of the top cricket nations in the world gathered in Australia and New Zealand to compete in the World Cup. After furious pool play, the top eight entered the "knockout" rounds.

All of the early games drew huge numbers of viewers, with the India vs. Pakistan match reaching 1 billion people. Then the knockout stage set new records. A record 630 million people in India alone watched the semifinal that India lost to Australia. The home teams

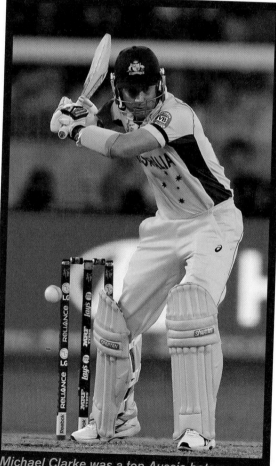

Michael Clarke was a top Aussie batsman.

TOP MOMENTS

* 4x100: That's what Sri Lanka's **Kumar Sangakkara** did when he had four straight games with 100-plus runs.

* **Chris Gayle** of the West Indies scored a rare double-century (more than 200 runs) when he put up 215 against Zimbabwe. ▶▶▶

* **Martin Guptill** of New Zealand did Gayle one better with a World Cup–record 237 runs in a quarterfinal win over the West Indies. Guptill ended as the tournament's top scorer.

* In the semifinal, New Zealand made its first World Cup final by scoring the winning run on the second-to-last bowl of the match.

* In bowling news, New Zealand's Tim Southee got seven batters out against England, tying a World Cup record.

* Ireland and Afghanistan are not considered part of the top level of world cricket nations, but both had big upsets in the World Cup. Ireland beat the West Indies, while Afghanistan shocked Scotland.

both made it through to the final match, which was watched by more than 1.5 billion people in nearly every country in the world.

They saw Australia outlast New Zealand, winning 186–183. **Michael Clarke** scored 74 runs, while **Steve Smith** scored 56 more for Australia. **Mitchell Starc** and the other Aussie bowlers mowed down the Kiwis, getting five of their batsmen to sit down without scoring a single run. In fact, Australia scored enough runs to win with only 5 of its 11 players needing to bat. It was the fifth world championship for the team from Down Under.

FINAL EIGHT

QUARTERFINALS

South Africa OVER **Sri Lanka**

India OVER **Bangladesh**

Australia OVER **Pakistan**

New Zealand OVER **West Indies**

SEMIFINALS

Australia OVER **India**

New Zealand OVER **South Africa**

CHAMPIONSHIP

Australia OVER **New Zealand**

Triple Crown...Finally!

Fans captured a moment of history as American Pharoah rocketed home to victory.

Horse racing's greatest prize was finally claimed in 2015. **American Pharoah** became the first Thoroughbred horse to win the Triple Crown in 37 years. Ridden by jockey **Victor Espinoza**, Pharoah (yes, they know it's not spelled right!) won the Kentucky Derby, the Preakness Stakes, and the Belmont Stakes. The challenge of winning three races in about two months defeated many great horses. Pharoah put it all together, though, and romped into history.

Kentucky Derby

Jockey **Victor Espinoza**, who used to drive a bus in his native Mexico, won his second straight Kentucky Derby. In 2014, he won on board **California Chrome**. In 2015, his mount, **American Pharoah**, was the favorite in the race, and the horse came through with a strong performance. Pharoah's trainer, **Bob Baffert**, earned his fourth Derby win.

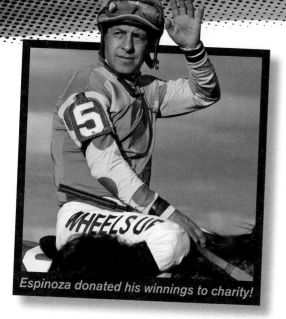

Espinoza donated his winnings to charity!

The horse's owner, **Ahmed Zayat**, finally got a first-place trophy after earlier horses had finished second three times.

Preakness Stakes

In racing, they call a horse that runs well in rainy, mucky conditions a "mudder." American Pharoah proved to be the best mudder in the pack as he won the Preakness racing on a thick, sloppy track in the rain. The drumbeat for the Triple Crown got even louder, as racing fans hoped once again to see history at the Belmont.

Belmont Stakes

The Belmont Stakes is where Triple Crown attempts go to die. Since 1932, 23 horses have won the first two legs only to lose (or not even compete) in the Belmont Stakes. The most recent was California Chrome in 2014.

Why is this race so hard? Because it is so long. The race, at Belmont Park on Long Island, New York, is 1.5 miles long. It's one of the last races run at that distance. Most horses will never race that much at once in their lives . . . except for this big event. A horse aiming for the Triple Crown has already run two tough races and now they face the longest one last. In fact, how many of the horses in the 2015 Belmont Stakes had run 1.5 miles? None.

American Pharoah didn't seem to mind a bit. Espinoza put his horse out in front early and never looked back. The horse won by 5.5 lengths (that means lengths of a horse in front of the next finisher). His time of 2:26.65 was the second-fastest winning time in Belmont Stakes history.

Jockey, horse, and a group of owners and trainers gathered in the winner's circle for a triple celebration!

TRIPLE CROWN WINNERS
ALL-TIME

2015 **American Pharoah**	1943 **Count Fleet**
1978 **Affirmed**	1941 **Whirlaway**
1977 **Seattle Slew**	1937 **War Admiral**
1973 **Secretariat**	1935 **Omaha**
1948 **Citation**	1930 **Gallant Fox**
1946 **Assault**	1919 **Sir Barton**

Winter Sports

A year after a Winter Olympics, athletes were still hitting the slopes and the rinks, adding titles to impressive careers or making their marks for the first time. Pull on your mittens and let's take a spin through the snow and ice in search of champions.

Speed Skating

With a solid final-day performance, **Heather Richardson** of the US became the women's Speed Skating World Cup champion. Her victory at the 500-meter finals at the event held in the Netherlands clinched her title. She also finished second in the 1500-meter event.

Bobsledding

Bobsled driver **Elana Meyers Taylor** became the first American woman to win the World Cup. She capped off her title with a win at a track in Germany during the World Championships. She was joined by pusher **Cherrelle Garrett**. It was the first world title earned on a track outside the US by any American athlete since 1959.

Ice Skating

Ice skating welcomed newcomers to the top of every medals podium. **Javier Fernández** used his powerful jumping ability to win Spain's first-ever world championship in the men's singles. **Elizaveta Tuktamisheva** won the women's singles for Russia, her first world title. The Worlds continued a hot streak on the ice for Tuktamisheva, who had won eight of her ten previous competitions. The rookie winners continued in ice dancing, as France's **Gabriella Papadakis** and **Guillaume Cizeron** won their first world gold medal. In pairs skating, Canada got its first gold since 2001 after **Meagan Duhamel** and **Eric Radford** earned the highest scores.

He reigns in Spain! Javier Fernández was the world champ.

Lindsey Vonn became the all-time leader in World Cup wins with another fantastic season.

World Cup Skiing

Fans of the top alpine skiing circuit might have thought they were seeing double. At the end of the 2015 World Cup season; the same two skiers who had won the 2014 World Cup were atop the final standings . . . again. In fact, Austria's **Marchel Hirscher** won his fourth straight World Cup season title. **Anna Fenninger** won her second straight championship. She's also from Austria, giving that Alpine nation a sweep of the top spots. Hirscher also claimed the slalom and giant slalom titles, while Fenninger won GS and Super Combined.

American star **Lindsey Vonn** finished third overall in the final World Cup standings, but did capture world championships in downhill and Super-G. She was coming back from a serious knee injury that cut her 2014 season short and kept her out of early races this season, too.

Vonn added another page to her remarkable career in January. She won a Super-G race in Italy for her 63rd career World Cup win, a new all-time record. The old record was held by Austria's **Annemarie Moser-Proell**, and had stood for 35 years! Vonn's mother made her first trip to Europe to be present for the big race. Vonn has established herself as the greatest woman skier ever.

At the single-weekend World Championships in Colorado, America's **Ted Ligety** won his third straight giant slalom title. **Mikaela Shiffrin** won the slalom at the same event, repeating her Winter Olympics success for the US team. American **Travis Ganong** also won silver in the men's downhill.

Tour de France

Chris Froome (yellow jersey, below) of Great Britain became the twentieth rider in history to own at least two Tour de France victories. The 2013 winner rode into Paris on July 26, 2015, ahead of the pack by more than a minute. He also became the first rider from Britain to win more than one Tour de France. In fact, it was not until Bradley Wiggins in 2012 that any rider from the United Kingdom had won the fabled race. Now, British riders have three of the last four championships.

Froome used his powerful climbing skills in the many mountain stages of the Tour, which lasted more than three weeks. He finished first in the overall mountain stages, which earned him the red-polka-dot jersey to go with his famous yellow jersey that the overall Tour champ wears. He was the first since five-time-winner Eddy Merckx in 1970 to with both jerseys in the same Tour.

Andrew Talansky was the highest American; he finished eleventh.

TOP FIVE

PLACE/NAME/COUNTRY	TIME BEHIND
1. Chris FROOME / UK	
2. Nairo QUINTANA / Colombia	1:12
3. Alejandro VALVERDE / Spain	5:25
4. Vincenzo NIBALI / Italy	8:36
5. Alberto CONTADOR / Spain	9:48

Track & Field

The winners at the 2015 USA Outdoor Track & Field Championships included a lot of familiar faces to track fans. Among the veterans who took home gold medals:

✳ **Allyson Felix** in the women's 400 meters. It was her first at that distance after winning seven 200-meter titles.

✳ **Matthew Centrowitz** in the men's 1500 meters. It was his third national title. **Jenny Simpson** repeated as national champ in the women's 1500.

✳ **Dawn Harper-Nelson** in the women's 100-meter hurdles for the fourth time.

✳ **David Oliver** captured his fourth 110-meter hurdles.

✳ **Evan Jager** earned his third gold in the steeplechase race.

✳ **Nick Symmonds** won the 800 meters, seven years after he won his first USA championship.

A new face captured one of the most well-known races. **Jenna Prandini** ran the

Future star? Prandini won the 200.

fourth-fastest time in the world in 2015 in the women's 200 meters.

All the winners and some runners-up from the USA meet qualified for the World Track & Field Championships (see box).

World Track & Field Championships

The highlight of the annual championships for the world's best runners, jumpers, and throwers came early. In the men's 100 meters, 2012 Olympic champion **Usain Bolt** of Jamaica nipped America's **Justin Gatlin** by 0.01 seconds. Gatlin had been the best in the world to that point in 2015, but at crunch time, Bolt kept his title. He added wins in the 200 meters and with Jamaica's 4x100-meter relay team. American decathlete **Ashton Eaton** set a world record in winning his event. It was a rare bright spot for US athletes, whose 18 medals were the country's lowest total since 2003. Kenya ended up tied with Jamaica for the most gold medals, helped by a final-day, come-from-behind win in the 1500 meters by **Asbel Kiprop**.

Lacrosse

The Rush and the Rock in a lax attack!

1,107

That's how many boy's and girl's high school lacrosse teams were added from 2009 to 2014, making "lax," as players call it, the fastest-growing high school sport in the nation.

However, after the season, team owners announced that the club was moving to Saskatchewan. It will retain the name "Rush." The NLL also announced that the Georgia Swarm will join as the league's tenth team.

INDOOR LACROSSE

The prize for winning the National Lacrosse League's 2015 title? For the Edmonton Rush, it was a move to a new city. The Rush defeated the Toronto Rock to capture its first league championship. **Matthew Dinsdale** snuck in a goal with just over a minute left to break a 10–10 tie. The Rush and goalie **Aaron Bold** held on during a furious attack by Toronto. **Mark Matthews** was the high scorer with five goals. It was the first NLL final between a pair of teams from Canada.

MAJOR LEAGUE LACROSSE

The leading outdoor lacrosse league finished its 14th season with a bang. The New York Lizards squeaked by the Rochester Rattlers to win their first Major League Lacrosse title since 2003. The Lizards didn't even have the lead in the championship game until the fourth quarter. The teams then traded goals until New York pulled away at the end to win, 15–12. The Lizards might have won their title before the season began, when they traded for seven-time All-Star midfielder **Paul Rabil**. All he did was have a hat trick in the final and win the MVP award!

The Big Fight

You always know when the Super Bowl will be. The World Series is always in the fall. The Kentucky Derby is the first Saturday in May. But boxing fans are often in the dark about when they will see the big matchups. Fans have been waiting for superstars **Floyd Mayweather** and **Manny Pacquiao** to battle for years. Both are considered the top fighters in the world at any weight. But they had never fought . . . until May 2, 2015.

For more than five years, the boxers and their handlers teased fans. Will they fight? Won't they? Where will it be? Who will get more money?

Finally, all the talking was over and the two agreed to battle in Las Vegas for the welterweight championship.

Millions of people tuned in (see Big Number box) and a packed house of celebrities watched at the MGM Grand.

Mayweather used his long arms to nail Pacquiao with jabs.

Mayweather-Pacquiao Fight Stats

	HT.	WT.	L/R	AGE	RECORD*
Floyd Mayweather	5-8	147	R	38	48-0 (26 KO)
Manny Pacquiao	5-6	147	L	36	57-6-2 (38 KO)

(*after their 2015 match)

$500,000,000

That's how much money was generated by the fight. Fans paid to watch on TV or watch in person. Each fighter took home more than $100 million for about 45 minutes of work.

The fight, however, did not live up to the long wait for it finally to happen. It was actually pretty boring. Neither boxer scored a knockdown. Both danced and jabbed, but without many flurries of punches. After 12 rounds, Mayweather won in a unanimous decision.

The big winners? The fighters and the promoters. The losers? Fans who waited so long and were mostly disappointed.

Pan Am Games

They're not the Olympics, but since they bring half the world together for athletic events, they sure look like them! The Pan Am Games began in 1951, connecting the nations in North, Central, and South America. The 2015 event was held in Toronto, Canada, with more than 40 nations taking part. Much like the Olympics, a host of individual and team sports were contested in many places around Toronto. Winners earned gold, silver, and bronze medals.

Many sports use the Pan Am Games to qualify athletes for the 2016 Summer Olympics.

Final Medal Standings

	NATION	TOTAL MEDALS
1.	**United States**	265
2.	**Canada**	217
3.	**Brazil**	141
4.	**Cuba**	97
5.	**Colombia**	72

USA, USA!

American athletes always do well at the Pan Am Games. Here are some of the other top performances by US athletes.

Swimming star Natalie Coughlin was golden.

⊙ American women dominated swimming, winning 32 medals, more than any other team. **Natalie Coughlin** earned four of those.

⊙ While the American men's baseball team fell to Canada in the final, the women's team took home the gold medal. They beat the hosts from Canada in the first-ever appearance for women's baseball.

⊙ In rhythmic gymnastics, **Laura Zeng** won five medals, the most by any athlete at the Games.

⊙ **Kim Rhode** set a world record in skeet shooting while repeating her 2011 gold medal.

⊙ The US women's volleyball team won indoor gold, defeating Brazil.

⊙ **Lorig Khatuna** won the individual archery gold medal.

Home Cooking

With their countrymen cheering them on, Canadian athletes had plenty to boast about at the Games held up north. The host nation won its most gold medals ever in the Pan Am Games, finishing with 78. Among the golden highlights:

➔ **Andre De Grasse** won the 100-meter sprint.

➔ Team equestrian gold!

➔ Men's baseball ended in a thrilling final game that Canada won on an American error in the bottom of the tenth.

➔ Canada won women's basketball, knocking off the favored US team.

➔ Six gold medals went to the women's swimming team.

➔ **Tory Nyhaug** won men's BMX gold.

➔ **Elizabeth Gleadle** fed off the home crowd to win the javelin.

The US led the way with 103 gold medals. The most came in track and field, with 13.

Yes, those are roller skates on winner Giselle Soler.

Medals for More

While the usual track and field, swimming, and soccer events are part of the Pan Am Games, the competitions also include some sports that don't get Olympic entry. So here's a spotlight on some Pan Am events that don't always get into the spotlight!

✱ BOWLING: **Marcelo Suartz** of Brazil and Shannon Pluhowsky of the US bowled for gold!

✱ WATERSKIING: Athletes competed in trick, speed, and slalom events. Canada's **Whitney McClintock** and Chile's **Felipe Miranda** were the overall winners.

✱ SQUASH: **Miguel Rodriguez** of Colombia defeated Peru's **Diego Elias** for the gold.

✱ ROLLERSKATING: **Marcel Sturmer** of Brazil was the men's free skate champion. **Giselle Soler** of Argentina won the women's event. And yes, it's like ice skating, but on wheels.

AMAZING SPORTS

SURF'S UP . . . AND BIG!

Dude! That is one really huge surfboard! A group of 66 totally rad surfers piled on to this 42.5-foot-long board in Huntington Beach, California. They stayed on it for about 15 seconds as the wave carried them to the beach. Guinness Records officials were on hand to declare it the most people ever to ride a single surfboard! Totally awesome, man!

Wild Winners!

People will compete in just about anything . . . anywhere. Most of this book covers sports and competitions that we've all heard of. The Super Bowl. The World Cup. The World Series. The Kentucky Derby . . . those sort of things. But now it's time to take a look at some events that don't get the big headlines, but are just as important to the people who take part in them. Watch your favorite sports website for more info on these and other wild and crazy sports.

Kabaddi World Championships

How long can you hold your breath? In India, Pakistan, and other Southeast Asian countries, Kabaddi is a popular sport. Teams of seven play a sort of tag (with a bit of wrestling), with one player at a time trying to tag members of the other team. The trick is that the tagging player has to chant "Kabaddi, Kabaddi" without stopping; that is, the player has to take only one breath. If that breath runs out, he's out

Can the Iranian player (in red) tag a player from India before he has to breathe?

and it's the next player's turn. The defense can try to trap and hold the player trying to do the tagging. India won the 2014 World Cup by knocking off Pakistan in a squeaker, 45-42.

Slacklining

Tightrope walking is for circuses and fairs. Slacklining is done much closer to the ground (about five feet) on wider cloth bands that bend and sway under the walkers. Contestants in slackline contests, such as the World Slackline Federation Championships, do tricks, flips, and spins. Judges rank them as in gymnastics. There is also tricklining, which is done at greater heights (30 feet or more).

Unicycle Football

It's football, played on unicycles. Players balance on the one-wheeled bikes (yes, they wear bike helmets) and play a rough version of touch football. A league in Texas usually plays a regular schedule, if they can get enough people to sign up!

Ice Climbing World Championships

Congrats to Russia's Maxim Tomilov for winning the 2015 Ice Climbing World Championships. That's right, ice climbing. Working your way up a sheer wall of solid ice using picks, claws on your shoes, ropes, and amazing bravery. There are competitions for going up fastest as well as for navigating the hardest routes.

Yes, These Are Really Sports ...Sort of

▲ The World Bog Snorkelling Championships are held every year in Wales. Swimmers plunge into muddy, sticky, stinky, bug-filled bogs wearing snorkels.

✳ Logrolling is part of the Lumberjack World Championships, which also include sawing, tree climbing, and ax chopping.

✳ Ostrich and camel races are held in Africa, Australia, and the Middle East. Camel races in some countries are done with robotic jockeys!

✳ Road bowling is a great Irish sport. Players take turns throwing a metal ball down the road. The courses go for miles, with spectators tagging along to watch—it's a sport and a day out!

better. The World Marathon Challenge had runners completing seven marathons, in seven days, on each of the seven continents. After starting in Antarctica, they ran in Chile, Florida, Spain, Morocco, Dubai, and Australia. David Gething of Hong Kong had the best time, but just finishing makes all 10 racers impressive. One was **Marianna Zaikova**, the first woman to go seven-for-seven.

◀ Free Climb to the Sky

The mighty granite of El Capitan, a huge cliff in Yosemite National Park in California, called to rock climbers for years. El Capitan had been conquered many times, but never via the challenging route called the Dawn Wall. In early 2015, a pair of hardy climbers got rid of that "never." **Tommy Caldwell** and **Kevin Jorgeson** spent 19 days inching their way up the rock face. They slept in bags attached to the mountain and ate food they pulled up with ropes. They finally made it to the top . . . and let everyone know via Instagram!

World Marathon Challenge

Running a marathon is one of sports' greatest challenges. That's 26.2 miles without stopping. In 2015, a group of courageous runners didn't go one better than that . . . they went seven

BOWLING BITS

* **ONE FOR THE KIDS!** Seven-year-old **Kamron Doyle** won the US Bowling Congress USA Trials in January 2015. He was the youngest winner ever, outbowling **Marshall Kent** 234-206.

* **PERFECTION:** It's not impossible—26 people have done it before—but consider how many millions of people bowl every year. So big props to **Hakim Emmanuel** who bowled three straight perfect 300-point games for a very rare 900 series total.

* **THREE FOR THREE:** They've rolled the lanes at the US Bowling Congress Open Championship for 112 years. But in 2015, **Matt McNeil** did something no one else had done. He won three separate national titles: singles, doubles, and team.

E-Sports

After growing steadily in recent years, e-sports powered onto the national scene in 2015. The biggest events were covered by ESPN and other big sports sites and networks. In fact, more people watched (online) events such as the Dota 2 International than watched (on TV) the World Series or the NBA Finals. E-sports: the future?

League of Legends

The most popular online game continued to draw millions of new fans in 2015. Like *Dota*, in *League* teams of heroes battle on an ever-changing field. They battle against each other in lightning-fast action that calls for speed, creativity, and experience to succeed.

A series of events around the world is held each year to send teams to the World Championships in November. In August, the North American League Championship series determined which team would represent this region, and the result was a bit of a surprise. CLG (Counter Logic Gaming) is one of the oldest teams, but had not won a major championship. This year, however, they powered through to the finals where they defeated Team Solo Mid. CLG headed to the Worlds to try to continue its amazing season.

Dota fans packed the Seattle arena.

$18,429,613

That's the total prize money awarded to winning teams at The International. The winning team got $6 million, more than the winners of Wimbledon or The Masters. Wow.

Dota 2

For the four or five of you who don't know, *Dota* stands for *Defense of the Ancients*, one of the most popular online games. Millions of people around the world are devoted to the game. Players use characters called heroes in a battle arena geared toward destroying the enemies' Ancient, which is actually a sort of fort.

The International is the game's world championship. In August, more than 20 million people watched as the Evil Geniuses from America upset CDEC Gaming from China. It was the first win by a team from the United States in the popular event.

NCAA Division I Champs

MEN'S SPORTS
(2014–2015 School Year)

Loyola Chicago won its first v-ball title.

BASEBALL
Virginia

BASKETBALL
Duke

CROSS COUNTRY
Colorado

FENCING (CO-ED TEAM)
Columbia

FOOTBALL (CFP)
Ohio State

GOLF
Louisiana State

GYMNASTICS
Oklahoma

ICE HOCKEY
Providence

LACROSSE
Denver

RIFLE (CO-ED TEAM)
West Virginia

SKIING (CO-ED TEAM)
Colorado

SOCCER
Virginia

SWIMMING AND DIVING
Texas

TENNIS
Virginia

TRACK AND FIELD (INDOOR)
Oregon

TRACK AND FIELD (OUTDOOR)
Oregon

VOLLEYBALL
Loyola Chicago

WATER POLO
UCLA

WRESTLING
Ohio State

WOMEN'S SPORTS
(2014–2015 School Year)

BASKETBALL
Connecticut

BOWLING
Nebraska

CROSS-COUNTRY
Michigan State

FIELD HOCKEY
Connecticut

GOLF
Stanford

GYMNASTICS
Florida

ICE HOCKEY
Minnesota

LACROSSE
Maryland

ROWING
Ohio State

SOCCER
Florida State

SOFTBALL
Florida

SWIMMING AND DIVING
California

TENNIS
Vanderbilt

TRACK AND FIELD (INDOOR)
Arkansas

TRACK AND FIELD (OUTDOOR)
Oregon

VOLLEYBALL
Penn State

WATER POLO
Stanford

Connecticut Huskies celebrate their field hockey championship.

Big Events 2015-16

September 2015

1–6 Cycling
Mountain Bike World Championships, Vallnord, Andorra

7–12 Wrestling
World Championships, Las Vegas, Nevada

7–13 Gymnastics
World Rhythmic Gymnastics Championships, Stuttgart, Germany

10 Pro Football
NFL regular season begins with a matchup between the Steelers and the defending-champion Patriots

11–13 Tennis
US Open final matches, New York, New York

18–20 Golf
Solheim Cup, St. Leon-Rot, Germany

24–27 Golf
Tour Championship, PGA Atlanta, Georgia

October 2015

4– Basketball
WNBA Finals, Sites TBD

6 Baseball
MLB postseason begins (Wild Card playoff games, League Division Series, League Championship Series, World Series)

8–11 Golf
The Presidents Cup, Incheon City, Korea

10 Swim/Bike/Run
Ironman Triathlon World Championship, Hawaii

23– Gymnastics
Nov. 1 World Artistic Championships, Glasgow, Scotland

31 Rugby
World Cup Final, London, England

November 2015

1 Running
New York City Marathon

20–28 Weight Lifting
World Championships, Houston, Texas

22 Stock Car Racing
Ford Ecoboost 400, final race of NASCAR Chase for the Cup, Homestead, Miami

December 2015

3–12 Rodeo
National Finals Rodeo,
Las Vegas, Nevada

4, 6 College Soccer
Women's College Cup,
Cary, North Carolina

5 College Football
ACC Championship Game,
Charlotte, North Carolina

Big Ten Championship Game,
Indianapolis, Indiana

Pac-12 Championship Game,
Santa Clara, California

SEC Championship Game,
Atlanta, Georgia

11, 13 College Soccer
Men's College Cup,
Kansas City, Kansas

TBA* Soccer
MLS Cup, Site and
date TBA

31 College Football
College Football Playoff
Semifinal; Cotton Bowl,
Arlington, Texas

College Football Playoff
Semifinal; Orange Bowl,
Miami Gardens, Florida

Peach Bowl, Atlanta,
Georgia

January 2016

1 College Football
Citrus Bowl, Orlando, Florida
Fiesta Bowl, Glendale, Arizona
Outback Bowl, Tampa, Florida
Rose Bowl, Pasadena, California
Sugar Bowl, New Orleans,
Louisiana

9–10 Pro Football
NFL Wild Card Playoff
Weekend

11 College Football
College Football
Championship Game
University of Phoenix Stadium,
Glendale, Arizona

15–24 Figure Skating
U.S. Figure Skating
Championships,
Saint Paul, Minnesota

16–17 Pro Football
NFL Divisional Playoff
Weekend

24 Pro Football
NFL Conference
Championship Games

28–31 Action Sports
Winter X Games,
Aspen, Colorado

30–31 Tennis
Australian Open finals

31 Pro Football
NFL Pro Bowl,
Honolulu, Hawaii

31 **Hockey**
NHL All-Star Game,
Nashville, Tennessee

February 2016

7 **Pro Football**
Super Bowl 50,
Santa Clara, California

14 **Basketball**
NBA All-Star Game,
Toronto, Canada

21 **Stock Car Racing**
(NASCAR) Daytona 500,
Daytona Beach, Florida

TBA* **Baseball**
Caribbean Series,
La Romana, Dominican
Republic

March 2016

28–
Apr. 3 **Figure Skating**
World Figure Skating
Championships,
Boston, Massachusetts

April 2016

TBA* **Ice Hockey**
NHL playoffs begin

2, 4 **College Basketball**
NCAA Men's Final Four,
Houston, Texas

3, 5 **College Basketball**
NCAA Women's Final Four,
Indianapolis, Indiana

7–10 **Golf**
The Masters, Augusta,
Georgia

May 2016

7 **Horse Racing**
Kentucky Derby, Churchill
Downs, Louisville, Kentucky

21 **Horse Racing**
Preakness Stakes, Pimlico
Race Course, Baltimore,
Maryland

28 **Soccer**
UEFA Champions League
Final, Milan, Italy

29 **IndyCar Racing**
Indianapolis 500, Indianapolis,
Indiana

June 2016

2–5 **Action Sports**
Summer X Games
Austin, Texas

4–5 **Tennis**
French Open, final matches,
Paris, France

9–12 **Golf**
Women's PGA Championship,
Sammamish, Washington

11 **Horse Racing**
Belmont Stakes, Belmont Park,
Elmont, New York

13–19 **Golf**
U.S. Open Championship,
Oakmont, Pennsylvania